Something
Furry
Underfoot

Something *Furry* Underfoot

AMY L PETERSON

ISBN-13:9781492759553

Cover design by Patricia Adams
Patricia@betaimages.com

Back cover design by Janet Lackey
janet@janetlackey.com

Book design by Maureen Cutajar
www.gopublished.com

Edited by G Miki Hayden, ghayden2@nyc.rr.com and
Alana Berthold, bertholdam@dishmail.net

Additional editing provided by a team of pre-release reviewers to whom I am greatly indebted: Aby, Brenda, Cindy, Dawn, Joyce, and Joy.

To the gentle man who was my father, for showing me how to spoil stray cats . . . and offering me one of the groundhogs in his backyard.

And to Mark for pretty much everything you'll read about here.

CONTENTS

Tip #1: When you marry someone who had pets growing up, chances are, you have pets in your future.

CHAPTER 1

The Unsuspecting Spouse

If my husband wasn't as cute as a yellow duckling, tenacious as a pit bull, and energetic as a kitten high on catnip, I wouldn't have a dozen animals in my house right now. But Mark exhibits all of that, plus employs the killer phrase, "I've always wanted one of those." He also knows how to blink his puppy-dog eyes, just so.

Back in 1994 when I was in the process of falling for Mark, I was attracted to his brains and his wit, but a bit distracted by the challenge of becoming a stepmother to his four children, ages three, five, 13 and 15. (As summarized in *From Zero to Four Kids in Thirty Seconds* by Amy L Peterson.) I was overwhelmed with the notion that I didn't know what I was doing and inundated by a panicky feeling that four kids were quickly taking control of my life. I had no idea that Mark was plotting to add animals to my sudden state of "duh."

Mark wisely began his quest for creatures by unabashedly using his children to get the things he wanted. He made use of this device for the first time on the way to our Lansing-area grocery store on a hot July day. Our plan was simply to escape from the children and our 600-square-foot apartment for fifteen minutes while we went off in pursuit of milk and macaroni and cheese.

At least that was the plan we'd agreed on *before* we left. So when Mark pulled into the local pet store instead of the grocery a half mile away, I said, "Uh, they don't have food for people at the pet store, honey."

"Conrad told me he always wanted an aquarium," Mark answered as he stepped confidently out of the car. "And they're half off today."

"And because aquariums are half off, that means we have to get one for Conrad?" I asked while wondering if "half off" and "on sale" would become words to be feared. I followed Mark inside to the squawking of birds; mewing of cats and kittens; and the thumping of rabbits, gerbils and guinea pigs. "It's not as if we have any extra money, with all that you're paying your ex," I added, thinking that an aquarium for Conrad now—in July—was a bit extravagant, especially with Conrad's sixth birthday just a month away.

It's hard to have a conversation over the cacophony in a pet store, and my comments went unanswered. Only later did I realize that was all part of Mark's nefarious plan.

Mark also knew that I was born with a propensity to imitate the noises of cars, animals, and pretty much anything else I heard, and that I would become thoroughly distracted in the pet store. And he was right. By the time I squawked back at a parrot, meowed at a cage full of kittens, and went "wheek, wheek, wheek" to some guinea pigs, Mark had in his hands an 18-by-7-by-15-inch aquarium with a lid.

I've never had a fear of lids before. But it suddenly occurred to me that lids are often meant to keep something contained inside so that the `something inside' won't get out.

Some of the more rowdy species of fish might need lids, I supposed, but I'd seen goldfish in open glass containers without lids. And the guppies my brother had raised in a small aquarium also stayed contained without a lid.

"So, is this for fish of some kind?" I asked clinging to my last shred of hope, as Mark took his receipt and change and headed toward the door.

"It's for whatever Conrad wants to put in it," Mark said calmly.

"Then," I stammered, "I want to state for the record that I do not do poisonous snakes, or snakes that eat mice—or tarantulas."

"Is that all?" Mark grinned.

With my B.S. in biology competing against Mark's Ph.D. in stream ecology, I was suddenly panicked by the terrible thought that I might have left out some major species of scary creatures. But try as I might, I couldn't put my finger on it. I worried all the way to the car, when some unexpected trace of maternal something-or-other kicked in again, and I reminded Mark that we really did need milk and macaroni and cheese.

We raced to get groceries and returned to the apartment chaos we'd left behind. Conrad, six, was fighting over a video game with Samantha, 14. Elizabeth, four, was pulling the clothes off her Teenser Water Baby, and Simone, the oldest at 16, was watching TV. Mark barked a few orders and the game ended, the TV went off, the baby clothes went on, and Conrad was handed the new aquarium.

Conrad's eyes lit up like fireworks and they got all big as if he hadn't expected to receive such a gift. Seeing this, I gave Conrad less than five seconds to think about what he was going to put in the aquarium and announced it was time to go catch a couple of frogs.

Our apartment was on a small, chemically correct lake that still contained enough marshy habitat for a few of the tailless amphibians. I hadn't caught a frog in fifteen years, but soon found that Conrad was quite agile at pouncing cat-like into the marshy muck. After two pounces, he came up with a healthy looking, green croaker and smiled proudly like a trophy hunter who'd just bagged a five-legged, albino moose.

Conrad held the frog around its waist so that its gangly legs hung down at muscular right angles, announced that it "would do," and carried it smugly back to the apartment. He lowered the frog inside the aquarium, added a small dish with water, threw in a handful of grass, and put on the lid.

"What are you going to feed him?" I asked.

He shrugged and walked away.

"Come back, my young man."

He turned, lowered his head, and stood there to take in my brief lecture on the unwritten household rule that one may keep wild creatures like frogs as long as the creature is well cared for, if not spoiled. "Your frog needs to eat. What are you going to feed him?"

"Crickets from the pet store?"

"You got money for that?" I asked.

"No."

"I didn't think so." I guided him back outside to catch some insects. As we headed out on our pursuit, Mark's parting advice was: "Frogs prefer live flies to dead ones." How helpful.

I never had a reason to catch an insect to feed another creature, but I'd once been bored enough to attempt to catch houseflies with one hand, and when that didn't work so well, with two hands. I'd discovered that houseflies are confused if attacked from opposite sides simultaneously and so shared this piece of lore with Conrad.

Catching flies is not as sporting as a moose hunt, and little glory comes of it, but I was rather proud of myself when I found a few houseflies attempting to warm themselves against the outside of the apartment, cupped both of my hands slightly, and swooped in for the grab. "I've got one!"

Conrad walked back to the aquarium with me and lifted the lid. I lowered my hands, opened them, pulled them out quickly and Conrad slammed down the lid. We sat back and watched as the frog turned around to face the fly. It sat for a few seconds as if figuring out what to do. I was beginning to worry about our froggie's understanding of the situation when it suddenly leaped across the tank, and mouth wide open, nabbed the fly.

We both said, "Wow!" at the same time. "Let's get more flies!"

Back outside again, I faced the apartment wall once more, and after a few failed attempts at a few flies, for the first time ever I wished that a housefly—or a flock of houseflies—would find our apartment desirable habitat so we could swat, pick up the still-fluttering body, and throw it in for the frog's eating pleasure. Obviously, catching flies wasn't easy, and I suspected that the big, green frog would need quite a few to stay alive.

Three houseflies later, Conrad and I had tired of the sport and I suggested that perhaps we should turn our attention to aquatic insects, my thought being that frogs hang out in the water and probably eat aquatic bugs. But Conrad had caught enough, he said, and returned to the apartment to play video games. When I called to Mark and explained it was his turn to catch some flies, he asked how many flies the frog had eaten. When I told him the number, Mark informed me that was enough for now.

Tip #2: She who takes on one pet successfully often ends up taking on more.

As I suspected, Conrad and Mark weren't very committed to catching flies or other insects for the big, green frog, and after working with Conrad to catch flies and aquatic insects for two weeks solid, I was tired of the sport myself and ordered the release of our captive.

Thereafter, a few other green frogs and a toad came to stay for a few days each, before a troupe of leaping leopard frogs appeared. We held captive eleven of them in all, and in an 18-by-7-by-15-inch aquarium, they seemed a little crowded together to me. I mentioned this to Mark, and he reasoned that if any of them started looking sickly, we would let a few of them go.

"What if one of them dies?" I asked.

"We waited too long to let it go."

Since feeding one green frog was a big task for Conrad, and knowing that the biggest leopard frog would outcompete the smaller frogs for food, I silently bet that the smallest of the frogs would only last one day. I didn't like betting against animals when it came to survival, and I didn't like the amount of time my brain calculated it would take to catch enough food to keep these frogs alive. Mark, who possibly was thinking along the same lines, ran off to the pet store and returned with a plastic bag crawling with crickets.

Mark handed Conrad the bag of crickets, then instructed him to remove the lid and open up the bag "and the crickets will just jump out." Conrad did as he was told, but the crickets didn't follow the script. Many of them poked their tiny feet into the sides of the plastic bag and hung on for their dear little lives.

"They know they're going to be eaten," I told Mark. "Poor things."

"It's what they were raised for," Conrad said matter-of-factly.

Then it happened. One of the crickets finally jumped out of the bag, and moments later, jumped onto a small twig Mark had placed inside the aquarium. In a flash, a leopard frog leaped at it and the cricket was gone.

We all went "Wow!" at the same time.

Wanting to see more of the same, Conrad tapped on the bottom of the bag to scare the other crickets inside the aquarium. But before the lid was secured in place, two crickets leaped out of the aquarium and onto the floor of our apartment. Conrad pounced once and returned the cricket to the cage. When the other cricket disappeared behind the sofa, nobody went after it, because all 11 frogs were leaping across the aquarium in pursuit of the crickets, and nobody wanted to miss watching the action. Some frogs launched themselves from one end of the aquarium to the other, mouths wide open, snatching up a cricket each before landing on the other side. When two frogs collided while going for the same cricket, I found myself cheering for the frogs.

Mark said, "That's the spirit," and patted me on the back.

It was then I realized how demented I'd become participating in this miniature world. I had been suckered into Mark's critter web and had responded exactly the way Mark had hoped.

That evening, I went to sleep to the sound of a chirping cricket.

Nobody ever did go looking for the cricket that had gotten away, because with six people in a 600-square-foot apartment, it would have taken us hours just to move the junk to begin searching for the little fella. And we had many

SOMETHING FURRY UNDERFOOT

other pressing things to do. Like buy more crickets.

The leopard frogs stayed with us for almost a month before we decided they were getting fat and lazy and should be returned to the outdoors before they were unable to catch anything but pet store crickets that happened to land within an aquarium's width of their faces. Mark and Conrad carried the aquarium outside and the frogs tumbled and hopped their way back to the wild.

After the frogs had been returned to where they belonged, Mark and I became "disoriented" (said he) while we were backpacking in Montana. *Disoriented* is a nifty word that gives the reader little hint that we wandered aimlessly in the mountains for five days. Mark spent three of those days with a fever and headache, not unlike someone with altitude sickness, and spent two of those days stumbling around rather like a drunk. He also carried a rubber raft on his back so that we could fish a lake that a map later showed was completely fishless.

We bought a house shortly after we returned from Montana, which was a trouble-free experience in comparison to our backpacking trip.

Then, six months later, with our possessions getting dusty in our new home, and the four kids only taking up every other weekend, most Wednesdays, and a few full weeks now and again, we felt so settled that our lives seemed predictable, organized, and rather dull. And of course, that's not a good thing for a guy like Mark.

**Tip #3: Beware the man who says his "son"
always wanted a certain pet.**

One day in late spring, I found myself being driven down one of many roads in the suburbs of Detroit doing a tour of the pet stores in search of iguanas allegedly "for Conrad."

16

"Funny," I said. "I never heard Conrad mention he wanted an iguana."

Mark didn't answer as he parked in front of a small store somewhere in the Detroit area off Eight Mile or Seven Mile or one of those other mile streets. We were making our way from a series of cages to dozens of aquariums, to a large enclosed room where iguanas frolicked away their time. That's when Mark stopped in front of a cage and said, "I love that Ostiletti chameleon. His bifurcated feet, independent eye movement, and that prehensile tail."

"I'm just glad Conrad doesn't want one," I said, dragging my husband away by the hand in the hope of getting our search over with.

"Oh, the iguanas will go home with Conrad to his mom's," Mark assured me. "And one of them will be taken to the classroom when school starts."

Suddenly, it hit me. This was June. The kids were coming soon for their usual month-long stay. So were the iguanas!

Then I saw them: a dozen eight-inch-long iguanas in a glass case, lying on top of each other and basically doing what iguanas do all day, which is nothing. My heart sank.

"Where's the saleslady?" Mark asked, his voice rising with excitement. "Those are the ones! Look at them. They're real fine-looking iguanas, nice green color, healthy."

"Thank goodness," I said. "And, in addition to being a healthy green, they come complete with sharp, pointy feet and nails, and beady little eyes that make them look dazed and stupid. And if you act now, you can get one of these marvels for only $19.95."

Ignoring me as he usually does when I become disagreeable, Mark ran off in search of the saleslady. Alone with the little lizards, I practiced voodoo, in the hope they would all die before I had to take two of them home. I had just cast the second aspersion against them when the saleswoman—a bubbly, do-good lizard lover—removed the two specimens Mark had identified as being the best of the batch. She handed one to Mark, then tried to hand me the other.

"No, thanks," I told her and backed away.

"Oh, come on, honey," Mark said, taking the second iguana from the saleslady. "They're real nice."

"So are poison arrow frogs, and I don't want one of those, either." I turned to the pet store woman to explain, "It's not that I don't actually like iguanas. I just don't need any as house pets."

Of course, my personal preferences didn't much matter. Later, at home, we stuck the two iguanas in a big, old fish aquarium that Mark had constructed in his youth. The aquarium was one of many items that had mysteriously appeared when we moved into our house. In fact, immediately following Mark's last trip to his "ex-house," the underside of our deck had suddenly represented the workings of a small zoo that had gone belly up: Stacked under the deck were several homemade cages, two aquariums, and several plastic containers with holes in them.

I soon learned that in his "previous life" with his first wife, Mark had rehabilitated a baby crow, raised turkeys, and had never been able to part with the aquariums he'd made when he was 18, "because you never know when you might need them."

With a tight-fitting, screen-like lid on the top of Mark's very old aquarium, the iguanas had plenty of air and couldn't escape. Mark then went about the task of chopping up lettuce, tomatoes, and other snacks for our new vegetarian pals, before turning his attention to finding out what he could on the Internet about iguanas.

The next day, we stopped in at our local pet store because

Mark had read that iguanas need vitamins and a lamp, the latter so that when the lazy lizards have nothing better to do—which is all the time—they can take in the light and turn it into vitamin D, which they supposedly need to maintain their lustrous "coat." I figured a lustrous coat might make for a nice belt, so I was all for it.

We asked the saleslady about vitamins for our new creatures and she asked how many iguanas we had and how old they were. Mark said we had two iguanas and told her how long they were since we didn't know their age. She asked if they were in separate cages, and when we said no, she suggested that we separate them, because when in pairs, one usually dominates the other, meaning, one might not get enough food.

All the more reason, I thought cruelly, *to keep them together.*

Like most Ph.D.s, Mark is skeptical of pretty much everything until provided proof, and he doubted that either iguana was in danger of expiring. "She just wants to sell us another aquarium and another light," he whispered.

"Yeah, I'm sure she doesn't really care about the animals," I whispered back. "She only works in a pet store."

We bought vitamins, a lamp, and some artificial grass, and returned with our new supplies so the iguanas could sit around and make vitamin D when they weren't competing for food. As I carried the new lamp into Conrad's room, I discovered the primary reason why iguanas are not desirable pets: They blow bits of food all over the place, poop everywhere, and knock over their water. "Other than all that, though," I told Mark, "they're very neat creatures."

By the time Conrad met his two new charges—which he named Frank and Izzy—his room had taken on the scent of eau de iguana. So I asked Mark to get Conrad to clean up after "his" scaly pals. It was not one of my better ideas.

Tip #4: The definition of the word "clean" differs greatly between the sexes.

See, a guy's way of cleaning up after iguanas is to take the artificial grass to the front door, shake it just outside the doorway, and let the poop and bits of uneaten veggies go flying. Call me picky, but the idea of my mother—who lives ten minutes away—stopping by and stepping in iguana poo and smushed food while entering our front door really rubbed me the wrong way, as did cleaning up such matter ground into my carpet. So, after sweeping off the front porch for the first and only time, I asked Mark if maybe he and Conrad could shake the stuff out in the backyard, say, off the deck. Mark coached Conrad, who waited until he was just outside the door before shaking the crud *onto* the deck.

Seeing that my indirect approach wasn't working, I handed Conrad the broom, told him to sweep the yuck off the side of the deck, and next time, to shake the yuck off the edge of the deck. "That way," I explained, "you won't have to sweep the deck off every time and then vacuum the carpet and scrub the floor when people track the crap back inside the house. Make sense?"

"I guess."

The other difference between males and females is that males just don't seem to have the sense of smell that females do when it comes to animals.

The smell of the iguanas reached overpowering for me after about five days. For Mark, cleaning up after the iguanas once a week or so was good enough. Hence, I became the resident Poo Tyrant. Every five days or so, I reminded Conrad it was time to clean out the cage again. As Conrad later described it, "When the Poo Tyrant said it was stinky, it was time to fling the crap off the deck."

Besides the smell, the other fun part about having iguanas in the house was the entertainment value when people like my sister, Aby, stopped in for a visit from St. Louis. Aby is a long-haired cutie with a business sense and a keen knowledge about what is normal to most people. As her polar opposite, I could think of no better way to engage Aby in all that was iguana than to allow her to interact with them.

To make this event the more dramatic for my sister, I had her sit on the floor with a piece of lettuce in her hand. "Like *this* is normal." She smiled oddly.

I called to Samantha, our second oldest, who entered the living room with an iguana on her head.

"This is just not right," was Aby's response.

"But it's not wrong, either," I said. "So why not feed him? This is Izzy, by the way."

"Like that matters," she mumbled.

As Samantha sat down with Izzy on her head, Aby's pupils dilated, her eyebrows shot to the top of her forehead, and I think she forgot for a moment to breathe. Perhaps more afraid to be called a wimp, however, she reached out to the iguana, and with the widest eyes I've ever seen, handed the iguana a piece of lettuce. Izzy reached forward and took it from her gently but with intent. Aby pulled back her arm as if she'd been electrocuted. "Well, that's enough of that," she said. "Thanks very much."

She stood, added, "Nice to meet you, Izzy. I can see you're a . . . a nice lizard," then turned quickly and ran off to the bathroom to wash her hands.

Since this had proven so much fun for me and the kids to watch, I extended invitations to my mother, father, brother, and a few select friends. Oddly enough, no one else was interested in feeding—let alone meeting—the iguanas.

The kids' month-long visit ended, and as with the frogs, the iguanas left our house well fed and lazy. Izzy and Frank both went off to a school, because it turned out Conrad's mom didn't care for pets of any kind, in a cage, or out.

I was drifting off to sleep on my first iguana-free evening when it occurred to me that my adorable husband had spent 20 years with a woman who hadn't allowed him to have all the pets he'd always wanted. Then I thought about the multiple cages and aquariums under our deck. And I knew some other creature was in my future; it was just a matter of time.

Tip #5: If your significant other was ever denied a pet in his/her "previous life," you may be in for a lot of fur.

CHAPTER 2

Goin' Hog Wild

The only time Mark ever bought a newspaper was when he was looking for pets, looking for pet advertisements, looking for pet shows, or reading articles about pets. Sometimes he'd actually read quietly, but most of the time he read descriptions to me as I was trying to write. In response, I usually just nodded or went, "Mm hm," and kept plucking away at my keyboard. After about the fifth animal description, though, I'd have to whisper, "Honey, I'm not buying you a . . ." and then filled in the blank. Usually, that would keep him quiet for a while.

"Oh my gosh," he gushed one quiet Sunday morning. "They have African pygmy hedgehogs at the local pet store. I've always wanted a hedgehog."

He hadn't taken up the topic of hedgehogs before, so immediately he got my attention. "You mean Conrad always wanted one," I said.

"No, I've always wanted a hedgehog," he countered, putting down the newspaper. "Besides, Conrad only lives here for a month in the summer, and when he leaves, so do his pets."

"Well, at least we've cleared the air about that."

I soon found myself at the local pet store, peeking in an aquarium containing several softball-sized balls of spines. The sign on the aquarium indicated they were, indeed, African pygmy hedgehogs. "Dynamic little critters, aren't they?" I commented.

When I turned to Mark for an answer, I saw that his eyes were watery and filled with "I want."

And then I was holding one—a ball of black and white spines that unwound like a pill bug and became a four-legged, soft-footed, pointy-nosed hedgehog with dark, moist eyes. It was the oddest-looking creature I'd ever seen. "And you want one of these things? Really?"

He took the hedgehog and held it up to his face. Without hesitation, the hedgehog stretched its pointy schnoz upward and licked Mark on the nose.

"What do they, um, do?" I asked the tattooed, hedgehog-loving salesman. "Anything?"

"Oh, they're great pets. They eat kitten food, can be litter trained, and they're real easy to take care of." He went on for a while like a politician, never really answering the question.

"You wouldn't rather have some fish?" I asked Mark, knowing as I put the hedgehog back in its aquarium that a hedgehog was certainly in my future. Mark confirmed my suspicion by shaking his head and looking at me like a little puppy in need of a good home.

Tip #6: Some pets are more interactive than others.

The next day, Mark and I returned to the pet store and selected one of the female hedgehogs, which we named Sonic.

We kept her in an aquarium for the two evenings it took us to design and build a large L-shaped house for her from plywood. We spent one full evening debating whether Mark's designed height of 12 inches was better than my design height of 18 inches, then began implementing his design. We finished Sonic's house by lining it with aspen bedding and adding a small "hut" that we made from chicken wire and papier-mâché. With a small tray of kitty litter, a water bottle, a hot rock to keep her warm, and a slab of plywood on the top part of her abode, Sonic's home was complete.

For exercise, we let Sonic run around on the floor for an hour or so of supervised time each day. Since our house is one continuous set of open rooms, from living room to dining room and kitchen and into the family room, Sonic had plenty of running space to exercise her tiny, fast-moving legs. To make Sonic's exercise time more like that of a real hedgehog, we purchased several of those lovely, black, plastic drainage pipes that farmers use to drain their farm fields. Sonic loved running in and out of the dark plastic and the pitty-pat sound of her happy feet more than made up for the hillybilly-like living room.

The funny thing about hedgehogs is that they can't see worth a darn. Sonic ran as if guided by a blind operator of a remote-control car, full speed until she bumped into something. Then she'd stop and turn or back up before running full-speed into something else. This process was both pathetic and funny to watch and made me wonder if the entire design of these little creatures had started and ended with their pokey spines. Over time she did figure out where things were, and even made direct shots into her drainage pipes without bumping into the sides first.

While Sonic's lack of vision was interesting, what I found truly weird was that she licked herself to produce a frothy goo of saliva which she spread all over her spines. It's called self-anointing, and while nobody knows exactly why they do this, one theory is that they do it in response to a very strong odor. It never occurred to me to stick a pot of boiled eggs in Sonic's face, or a blenderized mix of liver and onions, or a pair of my ripe athletic socks after an hour-long workout. I just know that on several occasions when I checked on Sonic, she was frothing up a good bit of slime and rubbing it on her body.

And that's about as interesting as Sonic got. We'd heard of other people who had gotten hedgehogs that actually interacted with human beings. But not our Sonic. She wandered aimlessly around the floor when she was free and spent the rest of the time alone in her hut, frothing herself into a shine and—or so I believed—plotting against me.

Tip #7: Most pets like to have pals to hang out with. Be careful what kind of pals you get.

On Sonic's second night in our home, Mark and I were sitting down for a fine dinner of cereal and milk, talking about how nice Sonic was, reflecting on the night we'd bought her, how she wasn't very interactive when she was out running into things, and how she was now alone.

"You know," I said before I could stop myself, "she had a buddy at the pet shop."

"Huh?"

Mark had been studying the details of something Captain Crunch was offering on the cereal box, so I went on, "At the pet shop the other night, all the animals were curled up and sleeping with a partner."

"Mmmhmm," he said, looking up. "What are you saying, my sweetie pie?"

"That maybe Sonic was taken away from her sister, and that, well, maybe she'd like some company."

In retrospect, it was one of the dumbest statements I'd ever made. Before I could even finish my cereal, Mark was on the phone tracking down a breeder in St. Louis, because "we don't want a male from the same litter as Mamma Hedgehog if we're going to breed them."

"Male? Breed them?" I sat dumbfounded. "Didn't I say 'sister'? And I know I hadn't referred to Sonic as 'Mamma Hedgehog.'"

Just how my desire to give Sonic a female buddy turned into a breeding opportunity for some stud from St. Louis neither of us can remember clearly. My only recollection is that Mark mentioned the possibility of making a small fortune in the hedgehog business: They were rising in popularity, and at two-hundred dollars each and the ability to reproduce every 32 days, "Well, just imagine," he said.

Since Aby was planning a visit home for Thanksgiving, a week or so later, she found herself heading our way with her boyfriend, Jay, and Louie, a spiffy male hedgehog.

The day of the big arrival, I received a phone call that began with the crackle of a bad cell phone and the words, "I think he's dead."

"Pardon?"

"I think the hedgehog is dead. He's not doing anything and hasn't done anything since we picked him up."

"In fact, they don't ever do much of anything," I started. Sensing her panic, I added, "Look, they're nocturnal and he's probably a bit stressed out right now. Are his sides moving up and down or in and out?"

"Just a sec." A crackle later and, "Yes. But he hasn't eaten anything or had any water since we left."

"And that was, what, four hours ago? I think he'll be okay."

Four hours later, Aby appeared at the door and, without even a hello, held a box to my face and said, "Here."

Mark took the box and opened it. Inside, curled up in a ball, was a brown, white-tipped hedgehog a few weeks younger than our salt-and-pepper Sonic. "He's perfect for the job," Mark said proudly.

As I took Aby's coat, she told about having to drive through East St. Louis—a town best known for its drug dealers—to get to the hedgehog breeder's house. How the breeder wasn't home, but his multi-pierced girlfriend said to come in though she didn't know a thing about hedgehogs. How Aby had to walk through this really creepy house, past a monkey and other exotic creatures, until she came to two aquariums with "these spiny, rolled up things." She then had to choose between three spiny pincushions and had agonized for eight hours afterward as to whether she had chosen the right one.

I assured her she had done very, very well.

After Aby posed with the hedgehog for the first and only picture ever taken of the two of them together, we let Louie run into things in the house before placing him by himself in a 10-gallon aquarium. Inside the aquarium was a tiny shoebox with a hedgehog-sized hole in it and some aspen bedding. It was meant to be a temporary home until we had time to make a new one for him. After another discussion about designs, of course.

At 6:30 the next morning, I went to peek in on Louie. He wasn't in the large part of the aquarium. I lifted up the tiny shoebox. He wasn't there, either. I called to Mark and we ran around the house with flashlights, looking under furniture, behind the refrigerator, everywhere we could think of. Because of a fugitive hedgehog, I was late for work for the first time in my life.

That evening, we searched for Louie once again. Realizing that he might be nocturnal, we shut off the lights and began the first of several nights of quality time together sitting in the dark on the floor, waiting for Louie to show up. Mark sat in the living room, I sat in the family room, and we chatted across the rooms about animals, kids, politics, religion, and sex. The latter conversation led us down the road of wondering how spiny hedgehogs mated without hurting one another.

Two more nights went by in the same manner: a husband and wife in separate rooms, sitting on the floor and talking dirty.

On the fourth night, we talked about getting another hedgehog. I was still voting for a female. Mark continued to like the idea of breeding.

And that's when I heard the pattering of little feet moving quickly across the floor. "That's him," I whispered. Straining in the dark to see our boy, I held still until the sound of the tiny feet seemed to be right in front of me. As I reached out blindly, I felt a cold nose on my leg. He'd run right into me. "Got him!"

Mark turned on the light and we checked out our little escapee. His eyes were brightly lit and he didn't seem any worse for wear from his adventure. We tucked him back into his aquarium with plenty of food and water to go on. And because hedgehog hunting wasn't part of what I wanted to do with my spare time, we put a small book on top of the aquarium lid.

The next morning, Louie was missing again.

Tip #8: Love always finds a way.

That night, we left a light on in the kitchen and waited yet again—Mark in the living room reading a book and telling me too much about what he was reading while I was trying to write at the dining room table. About an hour after dark, Louie emerged from the overhang of the cupboard next to the dishwasher. He blinked, lifted his head, wrinkled his nose, and ran off across the floor. When I picked him up, he curled into a ball and blinked at me with his tiny, beady eyes. This time, Mark placed six books on top of Louie's aquarium. I, meanwhile, duct-taped the underside of each of our cupboards. While feeling the underside of our other cupboards, I found a similar opening in the cupboards at the far end by the kitchen door and taped that up as well.

A few nights later, Louie figured out how to move his shoebox over to the spot where the books didn't quite cover the top of the aquarium. That night, we captured Louie a few minutes after dark. This time, we left only an inch of his aquarium top uncovered. I worried all night that he wouldn't get enough air to breathe.

The next evening after work, we returned to check on our hedgehogs, only to find that Louie was once again among the missing. After an hour sitting in the dark, we gave up on him. I turned on the lights so I could fill Sonic's water bottle, and as I bent over to get her bottle, I saw two bodies in her hut. Louie had scaled the walls—Mark's 12-inch walls.

I called Mark over and lifted the piece of plywood covering most of Sonic's box. We looked down at the happy couple, snuggled up next to each other. Mark said, "Way to go, Louie! What a stud." We let the happy couple enjoy their night of bliss and put Louie back in his aquarium the next morning.

The two baby hedgehogs arrived, like clockwork, 32 days later. They were about two inches long, blind and hairless, unless you count the dozen or so one-inch spines on their back. At birth, the spines were horizontal to the body, but within a few hours, the spines were erect and sharp enough for defense. In fact, for the first few days, it seemed the entire growth of the babies was directed to their spine production, both in length and in number.

As a new mother, Sonic didn't know what to do about those spines. On the first day, she stood on her tiptoes to nurse her pokey babies. On the second day, she stood on her toes and sucked in her stomach as she nursed. On the third day, I was about to find two pieces of wood to set her on to straddle so she could rise above the pokey spines, when she finally figured out that lying on her side was the better option.

The spiny babies grew quickly into round, spiny balls and soon looked like their parents except that they still had naked, pink tummies whereas their parents had soft white fur. The babies' naked, pink tummies matched their chubby pink feet, and I had to admit they were the cutest darn pokey things on the planet.

Cute as they were though, our hedgehogs weren't interactive like, say, the dogs of my childhood. And when they were ten weeks old, we sold the first two babies to unsuspecting friends for "a deal."

Now, in case you were worried about Louie while the babies were nursing and growing up, you need not have been. See, Louie got out every evening to run around our hillbilly living room, and every evening, we'd have to keep our eyes on him for a half-hour or so to make sure he didn't find a new hole somewhere in the house. Oddly enough, Louie behaved himself while the babies were in residence, never once trying to get out of his aquarium during that time.

But a few days after his children were gone, Louie escaped again from his cage and ended up climbing the walls to be with Sonic yet again. It was then I learned the true meaning of spontaneous ovulation and how in tune with Sonic Louie really was. In fact, it's because of Louie that we had four litters of hedgehogs, sequentially, none of which was part of any planned parenting on our part: All were because Louie continued in his role as dedicated escape artist.

We never did see how Louie was able to get out of his aquarium, and it was only by chance that we learned how Louie could scale Sonic's 12-inch walls. I happened to be checking in on our girl one evening, when I heard this noise not unlike sandpaper rubbing against very rough wood. I lifted the lid of Sonic's cage, expecting to see her rubbing against the sides of her hut. Instead, I saw Louie wedged between the wall of the living room and the wall of Sonic's house, shimmying his way up the crack like a professional rock climber.

I called Mark over, and we watched in wonderment as Louie wiggled his way up the last few inches before plopping over into Sonic's cage. He landed on his side, righted himself, and after running into a wall or two, found his way into Sonic's little hut.

"Should we watch?" Mark asked.

"When else will we be able to?"

"You're right."

Mark lifted the little hut and we watched Sonic greet Louie like a long-lost lover-hedgehog by touching noses. In seconds, the mating dance began, each circling around and around, first in one direction then the other. Then they got downright nasty, biting each other, spitting and hissing, until finally Louie mounted her. Amazingly, at that exact moment, Sonic's spines flattened out—in fact, so much so that Louie started sliding off of her. In response, he used his teeth to grab onto the back of her neck.

It was all over in a matter of mere seconds. They then settled down for a cigarette and a snuggle and whatever other romantic things hedgehogs do when humans aren't watching, and that was that.

Now, if you're thinking that Mark and I lived vicariously through the hedgehogs, well, that's not completely true. Mark and I are biologists and we study, learn, and use what we've learned at a later time. For example, later that evening, we played Louie Does Sonic, leaving out the spitting, hissing, and the biting. I must say, it was darn fun watching Mark shimmy up the foot-wide opening between the wall and our bed before plopping down onto our soft warm sheets. He was so sweaty it looked like he'd even done that self-anointing thing. Ooh, baby.

Tip #9: Breeding pets to make money doesn't always work out so well.

By the time the fourth batch of Sonic-Louie babies were old enough to sell, the hedgehog market had crashed, and they were worth only $50 each. When the last hedgehog took two weeks to sell, Mark finally conceded that his "get-rich-quick" scheme with hedgehogs was a bust.

"But," he grinned, "at least we broke even."

Tip #10: Ferrets are like two-year-old humans—they can climb higher than they can get safely down, they like playing in dirt, and they don't understand the meaning of "No!"

CHAPTER 3

Ferreting Out Another Want

Two years into my marriage with Mr. Biologist, I had successfully helped raise frogs, iguanas, and four litters of African pygmy hedgehogs. All of the critters had survived—at least while they lived with us. And in spite of the amount of attention given to our creatures, the four kids were growing and thriving as well. Life was good.

One Friday evening, Mark was reading a newspaper and suddenly said, "Hey, there's a pet fair this weekend at the Lansing Center. And it's only six bucks."

"What, pray tell, are you thinking about going to look at there?" I held my breath.

"I dunno," he said.

"You dunno? Well, I know better. You, Mr. Bargain, want to spend twelve dollars so we can go to a pet fair for the heck of it? I don't think so."

"Well, okay, I've been thinking about, well, maybe getting a ferret." That said, he hung his head and waited for the blowback.

"I see. And let me guess—you've always wanted a ferret."

He nodded.

"Whattaya know."

We arrived shortly after the pet fair opened at ten a.m. It was held in a convention center divided into two gigantic rooms. One room was dominated by dogs: dogs in dog shows, dogs jumping through hoops, dogs demonstrating speed ball. Another room was filled with cages and aquariums with all sorts of animals, ranging from sugar gliders to—Oh, lucky me!—ferrets. A dozen or more ferrets nestled together in a small aquarium, and from a distance they looked pretty much like chocolate-brown tube socks. Upon closer inspection, however, their beady eyes and long skinny tails made me think that someone had taken rats and stretched them from both ends to create these guys.

One look at all the skinny, furry, claw-footed ferrets sent me scurrying away to a quiet corner in dismay. I stood in resolute denial for perhaps ten minutes while Mark picked up each and every one of the dozen or so ferrets crammed into that small aquarium. The very fact that somebody would bring so many ferrets to a fair in such a small container made me feel as if I were breaking out in a rash.

The other thing that made me more than a little nervous about getting a ferret was that in the late 1990s, ferrets were still not common pets, and in fact, some people were deathly afraid of them. It wasn't until the year we were looking into ferrets—1997—that ferrets were added to the Compendium of Animal Rabies Prevention and Control, which gave a ferret that bit someone 10 days in a holding tank to hopefully not exhibit any signs of having rabies.

Unbelievably, before these guys were added to the Compendium, a ferret that bit someone was usually beheaded to test to see if it had rabies. And sometimes even if the ferret had been vaccinated for rabies, the animal was beheaded anyway because so many people were afraid ferrets carried rabies. The last thing I wanted was to fall for an animal, only to have it bite someone and be beheaded.

Mr. Biologist, however, was undaunted. "Boy, they're something," he said. "I sure would like one." When I hesitated, he added, "They come neutered and de-scented and with their shots. And, all you have to do is scruff them by the neck, and they go limp, so if they get into trouble—" He trailed off, perhaps realizing that the world "trouble" wasn't a word sales are made of.

I'd already told him I didn't want another pet right now, and that before any other pet, I wanted a dog. Yet I looked into his eyes, and he went blink-blink, and I knew. "But no lizards, tarantulas, spiders, or anything else, okay?" I pleaded.

Mark nodded, returned to the the furry clawers and claims he selected the one that didn't bite. "I named her Coco."

Tip #11: Some animals are on their best behavior when being inspected by a potential owner.

At home, Mark set up a cage he had raised a crow in many years before, while I watched Coco sniff around the spare bedroom. She sniffed one corner of the room, then as if controlled by an evil force, ran up to me, sniffed my foot and bit down hard.

A ferret's front teeth are very fang-like and create a puncture that's focused at two points, and quite painful. In a microsecond, I weighed my options: Remove foot from source of biting and fling tiny tube sock across the room, hurting, if not killing her, OR scruff her by her neck, which would immediately cause her to go limp. As I fought back a colorful array of swear words, what stopped me from hurling Coco's body across space and time and into a hard plaster wall was the notion that perhaps her pea-sized brain was too small for her to realize what she was doing.

In fact, in that instant of intense pain, I felt sorry for the creature inflicting the damage, for if she'd been properly bred, properly raised, properly handled, and properly cared for—if not spoiled—she wouldn't be biting me now.

I scruffed her by the neck. She released her hold. The pain subsided. With her limp body in my hand, I raised her up to my face so she could see I was serious and said, "Stop it!"

I was bending down to put her back on the floor again when Mark walked in.

"What are you doing?"

"Giving her my lecture about biting."

"She didn't."

"Yes, she did."

"I can't believe—"

As if on cue, Coco returned for another chomp, this time on my left foot. I used my right hand to pick her up, handed her to Mark and said, "Next time, let's shop around."

As I walked off, Mark said, "I picked up every single one! This one didn't bite!"

"She does now!"

Mark was also in denial about the cage. He thought he could keep Coco in the old crow cage, with its plywood bottom and screen sides that were stitched to a wooden frame at all points except one corner, which was held together with some Velcro. When I asked what would happen if Coco clawed her way out from between the Velcro, Mark said simply, "We'll have to go look for her."

While Mark never admitted that his response didn't demonstrate much sense of responsibility, within 24 hours he found himself at a pet store purchasing a ferret cage at my insistence. Such a cage has a lid, several sturdy sides, and a sturdy bottom, all made out of plastic-coated metal. Add a water bottle, triangular poop pan that is high on two corners, and a food dish, and we had a cage fit for a rambunctious ferret like our Coco. Put another way, we had a cage that I had always wanted for the ferret Mark had always wanted.

Because Coco came wired like the Energizer Bunny, each morning started with our opening the cage door so she could run around the house while we got ready for work. On the first day, she was relatively calm as far as tornadoes and tropical storms go, her sensitive nose checking out every inch of space that the bedrooms and main level of our house had to offer. By Day Three with our biting buddy, however, the smells were familiar to Coco and she began looking for other ways to entertain herself.

Little did I know that my stepping out of the shower would provide a source of amusement for both Coco and Mark.

The first time I stepped out of the shower while Coco was running around, she pounced and clamped onto my right foot before I had finished reaching for a towel. Once again resisting the urge to knee-jerk my injured limb and send the ferret flying across the room, I picked Coco up by the scruff of her neck, said "NO!" as if it mattered, and put her back down. Within seconds, she was on my other foot and biting again.

Mark named this dance the Ferret Jig. And the thing is, he liked the Ferret Jig. I was saddened by this, because in our first two years of marriage Mark had said he looked forward to my stepping out of the shower because he found my dripping naked body sexy; now, I was simply amusing to him as I danced away from the biting ferret.

Throwing a squeaky toy also resulted in Coco attacking and biting. Once I realized this, I bought a squeaky toy and took it with me into the shower. Before stepping out when I was done, I threw the squeaky toy squarely at Coco. This ploy worked—she went right after the toy, pouncing, biting, and making it squeak, the sound of which made her pounce and bite it again and again. Squeaky toys gave me enough time to dry myself, run into my bedroom, and shut the door behind me to get dressed without being bitten.

Oddly enough, though, I didn't like showering with squeaky toys or having to remember to find a squeaky toy before I stepped into the shower. So, I came up with the idea of using two towels after the morning shower: one to wrap around my feet and legs to keep Coco off me, and one to dry my body off. And though that worked, I finally told Mark I'd had enough challenges from Coco the Biting Ferret, and would he mind just waiting to let her out in the morning until I was dressed. He finally agreed, after calling me a wimp.

In addition to biting, Coco also showed us our first "weasel war dance." A weasel war dance is a spastic hopping around by an arch-backed ferret on tiptoes, going left and right, up and down, around and about, completely out of control. It is pure ferret exuberance. It seems to start out of nowhere and ends as suddenly as it starts. Sometimes it only took a simple, breezy flapping of a towel at Coco to get her hopping around in a weasel war dance; sometimes it took a treat like a raisin to get her going; other times she just started hopping around on her own.

> **Tip #12: Ferrets are curious little thieves that will claim everything as their own. Keep erasers, lipsticks, lip balms, balloons and other similar items out of ferret reach.**

I soon discovered that having Coco was very like having a two-year-old pirate, because she took any item of interest to her and hid it in one of many stash piles she created around our house. She'd dive into my briefcase and run off with a pencil, and—because erasers happen to be harmful to ferrets—I'd jump up from whatever I was doing and run after the fleeing pencil.

As I was tucking the writing implement safely away, Coco would dart back to my briefcase and scamper off with a pen or a tube of lip balm. She also sniffed out any shoes lying around the house, and, after biting them or gnawing on the laces, she'd drag them backward to her favorite stash pile. Until we got used to Coco, getting ready for work in the morning was a bit more time consuming than expected because we were often looking for a shoe behind the couch, behind the TV, or in "the ferret bedroom."

Between bouts of thievery Coco looked for other trouble to get into. One of her favorite pastimes was digging in our house plants. Because she could run quickly, she had half the dirt in our *Stephanotis* planter kicked out onto the floor before I could extract her skinny little body from the tangle of vegetation. And while I said, "No!" sternly as I had when she bit me, the admonition had no effect. As soon as she could get her fuzzy little feet back to the planter, she returned to digging in the dirt again.

Now I know you're probably thinking by now that I had nothing better to do than chase this whirling dervish and clean up after her, but I really did have other things to at least contemplate doing, so I implemented our first Anti-

Coco measure. We bought plastic lids, cut notches in them and strapped them to the pots with duct tape. In no time, our house plants looked like garage sale rejects.

With the plants no longer part of her personal playground, Coco turned her attention to investigating the cupboard under the kitchen sink and rooting around in the oh-so-enticing garbage. As with the plants, the first time I removed her, I said "No!", carried her to another part of the house, and watched her run directly back to the cupboard.

Not to be outdone by a four-legged creature that weighed less than two pounds, I found myself standing defiantly in front of the cupboard, arms crossed, and glaring at Coco. In response, she broke out in a weasel war dance and ran over to another cupboard.

A few days later, when she figured out how to pop out of the drawers connected to the cupboard and appear on the stove, I finally broke down and put rubber bands on the cupboard doors. I mean, really, those child-proof latches cost money and I wasn't about to spend money when something free would work. Of course, Coco wasn't readily turned away, and clawed at our cupboards in spite of the rubber bands. Today, the cupboards still bear our miniature maniac's artistic claw marks, which, when we finally sell the house, people will have to pay a lot more for.

Because Coco was such a little dickens, we figured it was only a matter of time before she tried to claw away the duct tape sealing her out of the underside of the cupboards, and disappear in the baseboards. So I spent another hour or so securing wooden slats with super glue, and being somewhat paranoid, adding duct tape just in case the super glue stopped working. The duct tape in the kitchen brought out the duct tape look on our house plants, so at least it all fit nicely together.

Oddly, we never did get the Good Housekeeping Seal of approval for our Anti-Coco devices. She also never did win over the hearts of the kids because she bit the kids whenever they tried to play with her. Conrad was the only person in the family who took a liking to Coco. He enjoyed the fact that she was devilish and he responded to her biting by donning a pair of leather gloves and a heavy sweatshirt and calling himself the Ferret Hunter. As the Ferret Hunter, he could go about the business of playing with her without any fear of being bitten.

Conrad also came up with a sort of great idea. "What Coco needs," he suggested one evening as he carried the biting, wiggling ferret back to her cage, "is another ferret to play with."

Tip #13: Two ferrets are often better than one, but sometimes one is better than the other.

Shortly after we purchased the ferret cage for Coco, Preuss Animal House, one of the local pet stores we frequented, also happened to have a newly delivered batch, flock, herd, or kit pack of 25 innocent baby ferrets. Or maybe there were 24 or 26 of them, I couldn't tell. It's nearly impossible to count individuals among a moving mass of fuzzy tube socks in a Plexiglas cage, hopping around, flopping on top of each other, rolling, and tumbling around.

When I stepped closer to the moving mass of fur, I noticed immediately that the ferrets were all small, firm-bellied little fellas with tiny tattooed dots in their ears. As if on cue, a saleslady appeared and told me the tattoos were applied by the breeder, Marshall Farms, which had been in the business of breeding ferrets for a very long time. She asked if we had ever had any ferrets and I told her about Coco the Biter. She assured me these particular ferrets didn't bite.

To prove her wrong, I reached into the cage and picked up one of the tiny fur balls and lifted it to my face. He was tan, had a pink nose, and a streak of pale white between his eyes. He had a chubby belly and appeared to be in terrific health. And not only did he not bite or even *attempt* to bite, he met my skeptical look with plaintive eyes that reminded me of Mark's when he saw something he'd always wanted. My heart melted on the spot.

As I held the little guy in my hands, I wondered if taking this ferret home would make Coco behave better, or if instead it would be like offering a sacrifice to the She-Devil Ferret.

I handed the ferret over to Mark, and when he held it to his face I'm not sure whose eyes sparkled more. Then the little fella licked Mark's nose. No discussion ensued. We carried the ferret to the counter, paid for our new charge, and named him Chunky because he had a nice, fat little belly. Chunky slept on my stomach during the half-hour ride home.

Because Chunky was tiny compared to Coco, we waited two weeks before introducing them to each other. Even so, it was too soon: The wiry, more aggressive Coco grabbed hold of Chunky by his neck and tried to drag him off behind the green recliner with her other treasures. This resulted in a high-pitched squeak not unlike a mouse squeaking into a microphone. It wasn't pleasant, and the only thing to do was to separate the predator from the prey by scruffing her. I'd long given up on saying, "No!"

We let the two ferrets play independently for a few more days before I finally took some of Chunky's bedding and put it in Coco's cage with, "He's here to stay, Coco. Better get used to it." As I put some of Coco's bedding in with Chunky,

I said, "I hope you have a lot of patience and some tough skin, little Chunky."

A week passed, Chunky got bigger and we reintroduced him to Coco. This time, Chunky dragged Coco by the neck for a few feet, and when Coco squeaked the loud mouse squeak, Chunky simply released his hold. After that, they must have called a truce, because they soon began pouncing and tackling and rolling around, with occasional breaks to steal from each other's stash piles. We never heard an awkward squeak between the two again. Within days, they even started sharing a cage and snuggled up together at night.

While we were relieved that the two ferrets got along, we were greatly disappointed that even with Chunky as a play pal, Coco continued her devilish behavior. The very first time I left her alone to play with Chunky so I could start a load of laundry downstairs, I returned to find Coco under a plastic plant cover, digging down to the bottom of the eight-inch pot.

At first, I could only laugh, because scolding and putting her in her cage had no effect. But when I realized Mark had just watered Stephie the *Stephanotis* and Coco had flung the wet dirt onto the carpet, onto the nearby wall, and into the cracks of the wood floor, I sorely wanted to shorten little Coco's lifespan. What stopped me was looking at her real hard and realizing she was wired with inherent nastiness and neither of us could do anything about it. I cleaned up the mess, alternately grinning and snarling, while Coco broke out in a weasel war dance.

Coco also pulverized an entire four-roll pack of toilet paper Someone had put out on the floor. No One knows who Someone is, but we are ALL quite sure Coco had fun.

This Someone also left a cardboard box on the floor crammed with tiny Styrofoam packing peanuts. By the time

I caught up with Coco, shredded bits of Styrofoam were clinging to every quarter-inch of her devilish fur. When rubbing her fur down the length of her body only transferred the Styrofoam to me and back onto her fur again, I decided the only way to clean her up was to vacuum her. With a naughty ferret in one hand and a vacuum cleaner hose in the other, I have to admit that I pondered the physics of sucking up the naughty ferret herself into the vacuum cleaner.

What I pictured was her immediate and surprised disappearance into the hose, an exaggerated wagging of the hose as Coco wiggled her way through the kinks in the hose, and then a lint-and-dust-covered fur ball exploding out of the bag with an unimaginable pile of dust. I shook the evil (and physically impossible) image out of my head and "thwrrped" each Styrofoam wad off her with the vacuum.

As much as Coco was a challenge to us, it turned out we didn't have to do anything to ensure Coco's speedy demise, because a couple of months after reaching a truce with Chunky, Coco suddenly became lethargic, as if all of her batteries had worn down. On the off-chance that the gentle Chunky had gotten aggressive and Coco wasn't getting her fair share of food, we put Coco back in the old wood-and-screen cage and left Chunky in the new cage.

The next day, when Coco was still not her usual self, we decided we better take her to our vet. Ferrets have such a high metabolism that without food or water for 24 hours, they decline pretty quickly.

Ferrets weren't popular in the Lansing area in 1998, and not many veterinarians there would treat them. After several inquiries, we finally found that the Waverly Animal Hospital would treat little Coco. An X-ray showed Coco's lungs were less than half the size they ought to be. The vet diagnosed juvenile leukemia, and after offering chemotherapy and other options that would have required a third job to pay for, admitted the prognosis wasn't very good. After one of the most interesting bite-filled years of our lives, we agreed it was time to say good-bye to Coco.

Before the vet took her away, Mark stroked poor Coco's head and said, "There were times I wanted to wring your naughty neck. And there were times I wanted to make a muff of you. But you were a good little ferret overall, and we tried to spoil the socks off you."

I petted her on the head and told her that she'd made my life pretty interesting during the last year, and if she came back as a ferret in her next life, I hoped Mark didn't select her for a second time.

As the vet took Coco away, I turned to Mark and said, "I cannot believe you told her she was a good ferret."

"Well I can't believe you couldn't say something nice to her before we put her down."

"She bit me more than a hoard of hungry mosquitoes."

"That's because you're a little sweetie."

Knowing he'd never admit he'd erred in his pick of Coco, I simply squeezed Mark's hand and guided his pouty face to the car.

Tip #14: A devilish ferret may not look devilish upon first inspection.

The problem with Coco's untimely death was that Chunky was without a four-legged play pal. During his play times—a half-hour in the morning and an hour or so in the evening after work—Chunky followed Mark and me everywhere.

I'm all for shadows, but this adorable one pounced on the back of my legs until I played, and was always underfoot when he wasn't in his cage. In fact, because he didn't make any noise, Mark and I had to walk around our house with our heads down so we wouldn't accidentally step on him, because unlike the Speedy Gonzales that was Coco, Chunky sometimes just loitered quietly nearby.

Chunky also trained us to give him treats by tugging at our pants legs or gently touching our bare legs. See, one glance in those tiny, moist eyes that made him look like the most pathetic little thing in the world and we found ourselves handing him a bite of this and a taste of that. After sampling various types of food, Chunky decided that tiny pieces of buttered bagel were his favorite, with frosted blueberry Pop-Tarts and raisins running close behind.

As enjoyable as it was to be Chunky's best friends, we knew something was missing for him and that was a ferret pal. So no more than a week post-Coco we found ourselves at Preuss Animal House looking at another litter of ferrets. In this batch, we selected an energetic dark sable ferret we named Rocky. Even though Rocky was much smaller than the round-bellied Chunky, he and Chunky got along instantly, rolling and frolicking around, and taking some of the pressure off Mark and me to entertain the incessantly cute Chunky.

At least for a few days.

The first Saturday Rocky was home with us, I ran downstairs to get some laundry and returned a few minutes later to find Rocky underneath the duct-taped lid covering a plant, digging and rolling around in the sweet smelling dirt. Just like Coco. The plant had been recently watered, of course, so the dirt was splattered against the wall, on the floor, and all over Rocky. I yelled, "Hey you!" which for some reason, resulted in Rocky's crawling his way out of the plant and onto the floor. He looked like a hairy, dirt-covered tube sock. After he shook himself off, he broke out in a weasel war dance. Just like Coco.

Now, I couldn't just throw Rocky into the washing machine like I would a hairy, dirt-covered tube sock (though the thought did cross my mind). Instead, while Mark held Rocky over the kitchen sink by the scruff of his neck, I washed him down like a giant, fuzzy kielbasa. After gently rubbing the water down to Rocky's tail, I dried him off in a small towel and placed him on the floor where he broke out into another weasel war dance, shaking, wiggling, and rolling around to dry himself.

"Unfortunately," I told Mark. "I think he might have enjoyed all that. Playing in the dirt, the bath, everything."

"It's almost as if Coco left a little note behind with instructions on how to destroy the house," he mused.

I had wondered the same thing, because when Rocky wasn't attacking plants we *thought* we'd adequately ferret-proofed, he was wiggling his way into my La-Z-Boy, pulling himself under the wimpy fabric stapled between the slats that make up the wooden frame, and clawing his way inside the stuffing. Once inside the chair, he'd claw and roll around, and throw out bits of the nice fuzz that made up the inside of my once comfortable chair.

The chair had been a gift to me from Mark and I'd never had the heart to tell him that since I had spent so many years alone in all sorts of chairs made to hold one person, I'd rather sit on a couch or loveseat with him. So, while Rocky slowly destroyed the chair from the inside out, part of me was actually rooting for Rocky to do away with the last semblance of my single days.

The thing about a ferret inside a La-Z-Boy chair is that it's not easy to retrieve said ferret without contorting one's arm into odd shapes or turning the chair upside down and risking injury to the ferret. And because anyone who might recline in the chair while the ferret was inside would almost surely end up killing the ferret, I found myself sitting down on the floor waiting for Rocky to emerge. It reminded me of waiting for Louie the hedgehog to appear except that I knew where Rocky was and Mark wasn't in an adjacent room saying sexy things to me.

When Rocky finally came out ten minutes later, I scruffed him by the neck, put him gently in his cage and set about the thirty-minute chore of ferret-proofing my recliner. That was a horrifying task because working fulltime and having a few animals made it such that dusting and cleaning were rather low on my list of things to do.

In the armchair, I found dust balls deserving of awards, and because the underside of the chair was a ferret stash pile, I also found dried Pop-Tart bits, a rubber ball, a vinyl key ring, and a few marbles that had come loose from my own head. I cleaned up the grossities, vacuumed, and then added a half-roll of duct tape to the underside of the chair to at least slow Rocky down the next time he tried to climb inside. Thirty minutes later, I flipped the chair back to its normal position.

Rocky also helped keep our interior decoration at the low level Coco had taken it to. Rocky proved that ferrets love diversity—of smells and sights and textures—and believed a closed door was simply a barrier that needed to be overcome. It turns out the easiest way to try to get under a door is to dig up the soft, fuzzy, 12-year-old carpet underneath. Our lovely beige carpet was soon shredded into bits and pieces as Rocky clawed a V-shaped notch down to the wooden plywood below our bedroom door.

This alteration was soon followed by a similar bare patch of carpet carved out below the spare bedroom door, and another triangular lump missing from beneath the bathroom door. The carpeting was admittedly pretty bad stuff, and some people credit Rocky with recognizing before we did that the floor covering needed to be replaced.

Now, you might be thinking that having chunks of carpet missing outside our doors was embarrassing for us when people stopped over. But we simply never had people over, except for family. So, unless my mother shared this secret with a few dozen seniors during her daily exercise class at the nearby mall, nobody else knew we had chunks of missing carpeting, duct tape on our plants, duct tape holding the wooden slats in place under our cupboards, and a fine variety of rubber bands keeping our cupboards closed. Until now.

Tip #15: It is possible to spend an arm and a leg to save a ferret.

All was well in Ferretville with our devilish Rocky and round-bellied Chunky, until one evening when we returned from work to find Chunky lying motionless in his cage. He was warm and lethargic, a sure sign that something was quite seriously amiss. Because of Coco's diagnosis, we immediately feared juvenile leukemia. Unlike with Coco's early demise, the thought of losing Chunky deeply bothered us.

The Wallet Opening Ceremony began at the Waverly Animal Hospital, where the ferret-loving vets ran a blood test, put Chunky on a teeny, tiny I.V. and gave him one antibiotic after another. Five days and $500 later, they called and said they couldn't figure out what was wrong with Chunky, and recommended that we take Chunky to a second vet in Westland, a two-hour drive away.

At this point in our marriage, Mark was paying about $1,000 a month in child support and child care costs in addition to half of all child medical expenses. We drove two older model cars, lived in a modest house, and were constantly struggling to make credit card payments. Five hundred dollars seemed like a lot of money for a creature that weighed less than two pounds. Yet, looking into Chunky's sorrowful eyes and thinking of the joy he'd given us, Mark and I agreed we couldn't just give up. So we held a second Wallet Opening Ceremony.

Five days and $700 later, the Westland vet called to tell us to pick Chunky up so he could die at home. They, too, had not been successful in figuring out what was wrong with our buddy after doing pretty much the same stuff that the Waverly vets had done, but also including the last-ditch effort of opening Chunky's tiny tummy to see if perhaps he had eaten something the X-rays failed to detect.

Now, the very idea of being charged $1,200 after two Wallet Opening Ceremonies, neither of which resulted in a diagnosis or cure for Chunky, ticked Mark and me off in equal proportion to the idea that it would take us more than six months to pay off the bills. But what was truly upsetting was the fact that the vets had given up on Chunky and had suggested he would die. That meant Chunky would no longer be with us. And we loved Chunky like nobody else had ever loved a little ferret before.

Our $1,200 did buy us several cans of special, soft canned food, and from the moment we got Chunky home at 8:00 that evening, Mark and I took turns feeding him the special food every four to six hours around the clock. At ten o'clock, Mark crammed a couple of wads of food into Chunky's mouth, dribbled some water off his finger, and watched Chunky—eyes half closed—go through the motions of pretending to be alive. Mark tucked Chunky into my old, heavy-weave Michigan State University sweatshirt and we went off to bed.

At two a.m., I awoke to feed Chunky. I was stumbling, mumbling, and feeling really out of it. And I was very afraid Chunky would be dead. When I opened the cage door and called to him, he didn't respond. When I poked him and still got no response, I panicked. With tears streaming like a waterfall, I ran off to tell Mark that I thought Chunky was dead.

Mark leaped out of bed, stood in front of the cage, stuck his finger into the can of food, gently propped Chunky's mouth open and said, "Listen, we just spent $1,200 on you, so you WILL EAT!"

The man who had said he always wanted a ferret was now my spectacled hero in tropical-fish boxer shorts and sporting a Kewpie-doll curl on top of his head. As I was admiring the cute man I had married, a very sleepy looking Chunky lifted his head from the sweatshirt, opened his mouth and licked two bites of food off Mark's fingers. A few drops of water later, Mark was satisfied Chunky would survive at least until the very next feeding.

At six a.m., Mark got up and forced Chunky to eat a little more. Four hours later, I took a long lunch from work, drove home, pulled back the folds of the sweatshirt, pried open Chunky's mouth, and with tears pooling in my eyes, fed Chunky about six bites of food. Five hours later, we fed him again and this time his eyes were open when we peeled back the sweatshirt. Mark then gingerly untangled him from the messed-up sweatshirt, which I added to the laundry. I found two other old sweatshirts, cut the arms off so Chunky wouldn't get stuck in an arm, and he nestled back down again.

Two days later, Chunky poked his head out from the sweatshirt to greet me. I stroked his little head and told him I was glad he was serious about this thing called living, and told him not to worry about the fact that Mark was teaching at night at the local community college to help pay off the vet bill. I chatted with Chunky, and all the while, he ate a quarter of a can of his special food and slurped a bunch of water.

"You know, we could maybe make some money," I told Chunky, "if we hung up a sign outside the house that said, `SEE THE WORLD'S MOST PATHETIC FERRET.' Cuz you're it, Chunky." I looked at him for a response, and when I saw his shrunken face; his sad, faraway gaze; his teeny, tiny tongue lapping at the water, I stopped picking on him. Suddenly feeling terrible, I explained, "You're the best ferret in the whole world, and I would never have anybody come over to see you like this. Unless they offered me $1,200."

Apparently Chunky forgave me, because within two weeks he was strong enough to drag himself across the cage to the door, eat what we fed him from our fingers and drag himself back to the poop pan at the back of the cage. As I watched him drag his back legs, it occurred to me that he might have fallen and broken his back. I hoped for another miracle: that Chunky would walk on all four legs again.

Mark and I continued the every four-to-six-hour feedings for about five weeks before I hit a physical wall from the interrupted sleep and working extra hours to make up for the long lunches I took to feed Chunky. I told Chunky he better start eating off a plate, because the days of my hand-feeding him were at an end. And when he looked up at me with those tiny, sad eyes, I told him that he was cute, that I loved him, but that I was serious. He apparently heard, because by eight that evening, Chunky's plate was empty, and the water in his tiny bowl was half gone.

After six weeks, I carefully put Chunky on a soft expanse of carpet that needed to be cleaned and replaced—which I'm sure you realize now could be just about anywhere in our house—and watched as he tried to move his back two legs.

His back legs didn't do anything, though, and he simply dragged his entire back half around on the floor using his good front legs.

That got me to thinking about physical therapy and wondering what kind of money I could make being a physical therapist for injured ferrets. When the answer was *not much*, I took Chunky's back legs and very, very gently moved them so they bent. He didn't wince or wiggle or try to drag himself away, so, satisfied that I wasn't hurting him, I moved them back to their original position. Slowly, I did it again, bending legs that hadn't been bent for quite a while, then letting them go back to their resting position.

For several days, I did physical therapy twice a day, and at no time did Chunky give me any indication that what I was doing was painful at all. Of course, the fact that he'd never peeped, squeaked, whined, cried, or made any noise of any kind when he was on his death bed gave me little confidence as I gently bent and straightened his pencil-thin legs.

And it's not as if I could call a knowledgeable vet within a 120-mile radius to ask if I was doing anything wrong. Moreover, in 1998, "Googling" wasn't an option, either, let alone a word. All I could do was ask Dr. Mark, who agreed that if it didn't seem to hurt Chunky, it possibly might help. That got me back to wondering how I would know if I was hurting Chunky, which got me worried all over again.

Luckily, a few days after starting physical therapy, Chunky cautiously put weight on his back legs for just a moment, though his legs then flopped back down, and he returned to the front-body pull that allowed him to move around. At the end of the physical therapy that day, I lifted Chunky to his four feet, and for a brief moment again, he stood on all fours. I cheered. He collapsed to the floor. I booed. And then felt bad.

A few days later, Chunky had enough strength to stand on his back legs for a few seconds. Then he took a step! I was so happy, I cheered, and a tear fell down my face. Day after day, Chunky progressed from one step to several, to slowly walking his way around the dirty carpet, which, I reminded him, other owners might have replaced in lieu of the same cost in veterinarian bills.

A total of 11 weeks after Chunky was given up for dead by two veterinarians, he was completely recovered and walking on all fours. His little tummy never got round and chunky again, but all parts of his personality remained, including his penchant for begging for morning bagel bites, Pop-Tarts, and raisins with a gentle pawing of our legs and the most pitiful look in his tiny, sad eyes. A total of 16 weeks after initially going to the first vet, Chunky broke out in a weasel war dance. I joined in, doing the Coco-inspired Ferret Jig.

There was one more thing to do for Chunky: Since Mark and I were fairly certain Chunky had fallen in his cage and broken his back, we added large pieces of plywood to each of the three levels of his cage so that the furthest he could fall was only four inches. We also added more towels and old sweatshirts to help break any future tumbles and reduced the fall to just two inches.

All was well again in Ferretville.

But I should have known otherwise.

One evening, shortly after Chunky was completely recovered, Mark and I were sitting at the kitchen table. We were both paying bills and lamenting the fact that we might have wasted $1,200 because if Chunky really had broken his back, there probably wasn't anything the vets could have done for our pal, anyway. I went on to say that I felt bad for having put Chunky through all that medical `care,' especially the operation. Mark agreed, and without pausing said,

"There's a ferret show in Lansing this weekend."

"You've probably always wanted to go to a ferret show." I smiled.

He nodded.

"Imagine that."

Tip #16: Some people are willing to drive a long way to get a ferret.

Considering our local pet stores occasionally had moving piles of baby ferrets for sale, it seemed ludicrous to me to drive across town a half-hour and spend twelve dollars at a ferret show to look around a motel filled with ferrets. But of course, we went.

The halls of the motel were lined with cages of ferrets, aquariums filled with ferrets, ferrets in tubs, and ferrets in just about every kind of containerized and cage-like contraption known to man. Between cages of real, living ferrets were small booths with stacks of folded cages, ferret food (with free samples), ferret lotion and ointments and vitamins, specialty carpet cleaners that removed stains and odor, and—my personal favorite—a booth with ferret clothes and leashes.

I kept trying to guide Mark along the row of cages and point out the cute stuff like sacks and ferret clothes and other ridiculous and frivolous things ferrets didn't need, with, "Oh, look at this. Chunky needs a top hat and tuxedo, don't you think?" Moments later, "Hey, look at this pricey leash and harness. Rocky might love to be taken for a walk outside."

Distracting Mark from the real object of his attention worked for perhaps 15 minutes before he saw what he wanted to see—a gigantic ferret weighing about five pounds and sprawled out like a four-inch-diameter piece of sausage in its owner's arms. The ferret was twice the size of our ferrets. And Mark was in love. He talked with the giant ferret's owner, Vicki McKinney, a breeder from Maryland, found out about an upcoming litter, and reserved one for us to pick up in July. From Maryland.

In April, Mark received a photograph of "our boy" from Vicki and a note saying that we could pick him up in about ten weeks. Mark hung the photo on the refrigerator and showed it to anyone who happened to stop by, meaning my mother was shown the photo of "our boy" a half-dozen times.

Mom acted all impressed the first two times, but the next three times she reminded Mark that he'd already shown her the photo and politely added, "You must really be excited about this ferret." The last time she just shook her head and said, "I know *I'll* be glad when this ferret is in your possession so I don't have to look at its picture anymore." Mark pouted for days.

On the Friday of the Fourth of July weekend in 1998, Mark and I drove from Michigan to Maryland and back for Tuffy, our soon-to-be-giant ferret. As Mark explained it, we spent $1,200 to pick Chunky up, so at $225—plus gas and a motel room and food—Tuffy, the part English ferret, was a bargain.

But even bargains get expensive.

See, Mark determined that since Chunky and Rocky were already pals, Tuffy needed a pal of his own. Mark claims it was my idea to get a fourth ferret, but let's face it, at this point in my marriage I was rather like a bobblehead doll when Mark said he wanted something. And even if I hadn't suggested it, he'd have wanted it anyway.

No matter who was at fault, we learned Preuss Animal House was out of ferrets, and found ourselves at Soldan's

Feed and Pet Supplies, holding a half-grown ferret with white feet, which we named Sox. He was about 12 weeks old and had been all alone in a small cage from about the age of five weeks. He was already big enough and old enough to be introduced to our other ferrets.

And what a big hit that wasn't. Sox sniffed each of his new male companions one after the other as if to acknowledge them, then immediately turned his attention to our new collection of Beanie Babies.

See, when not collecting live animals, Mark and I had been bitten with the Beanie Baby bug—er, obsession—and our collection occupied an entire bookshelf. We'd even left work early several times to drive over 50 miles when we'd heard a certain Beanie Baby was being released. To make sure our drive was worth our while, we pushed and shoved grandmothers claiming they were collecting for their grandchildren and kids who should have been in school, to ensure we got the Beanie we had driven—and were driven—to get.

In addition to the full bookshelf, we had a few hundred other Beanies hither and yon in the messy dwelling we called home. Buying and selling the Beanies was another of Mark's make-money schemes, whose ending would, like the outcome with the hedgehogs, allow us to break even. (We eventually gave most of the toys to charities.)

But back when Sox first entered our lives, we had Beanies upon Beanies. And the problem with an obsessive ferret owned by obsessive Beanie Baby collectors is that while the obsessive ferret was trying to take and hide the Beanie Babies, the obsessive owners were trying to prevent Beanies from getting bent tags, because Beanies with bent tags weren't worth as much as those in prime condition.

So, while at first we were willing to watch Sox jump up and pick his favorite-of-the-day and pluck it off the shelf and haul it behind a chair, when we realized that one particular Derby the Horse might be worth more than the six dollars we'd paid for it if its tag wasn't bent, we rounded up Derby and his pals from behind our furniture, doubled up the Beanies on the upper shelves and put books on the bookshelf in place of the Beanies.

We did, however, sacrifice three Beanies for Sox and went so far as to fling them from one corner of the house to the other so that he could once again engage in the pillaging, plundering and stashing he so enjoyed, mischievous little fella that he was.

While Sox was wrestling Beanies, Rocky continued to take vengeance on the carpet, the latest layer of duct tape on the underside of the La-Z-Boy chair, and the duct-taped plant covers. Meanwhile, Tuffy—or Big Wuzzy as we later called him—ran out from behind a piece of furniture and attacked like a cat, throwing himself at any legs haplessly walking by, then celebrating another successful assault with a weasel war dance.

When Big Wuzzy wasn't pouncing on us, he'd claw open a rubber-banded cupboard, climb over our pots and pans, pull himself up into the drawer holding our kitchen towels, wiggle his way to the front of the drawer, and push open the drawer with his front feet. Naturally, I responded by placing a ferret treat, Pop-Tart, or raisin in his mouth and shutting the drawer. Big Wuzzy ate the treat in the darkness of the drawer and pushed the drawer open again. I gave him another treat and shut the door. I loitered for a third round, and when he opened the drawer a fourth time, I carefully extracted him from the drawer and put him on the floor to go hopping off to play with his pals.

Only after showing this trick to my mother did it occur to me that this was not normal.

"Aren't you worried about him getting your pots and pans dirty?" she asked, her eyebrows raised in distress.

"Not really. I mean, most things we cook get boiled or fried, so—."

"You don't wash the pots before you cook?"

"Of course we do, Mom," I declared, suddenly wondering if rinsing and washing were really comparable.

"What about the kitchen towels?" she asked.

"Well, we do occasionally wipe old Pop-Tart bits onto a cleaned pot or pan—." I stopped when I saw her horrified look. "Maybe it's not such a good idea, showing you these fun ferret tricks."

"Maybe I'll not be eating dinner at your house."

"Maybe I won't invite you."

And then we both smelled it—the nasty, pungent, musky smell that one might associate with a muskrat, weasel, fox, and a dozen other musky creatures all "breaking wind" at the same time. Big Wuzzy wasn't supposed to be able to make such an offensive gesture, because all ferrets were supposed to be de-scented. But BigWuzzy could. And when he let loose, there was nothing to do except fling the doors open, turn the fans on, and put up a giant "DO NOT DISTURB" sign outside our front door, all the while hoping that for the next 24 hours, nobody showed up unannounced.

My mother's presence during one of these events was really rather disconcerting: After she wriggled her nose, she covered it with her shirt and exposed her little white belly, which caused Mark to raise his eyebrows up and down, which was just too much. I guided my mother outside, claiming that stronger old ladies than she had died when they'd breathed too much of the repugnant smell. Her parting words were: "Thanks for having me over. I had a blast." She pinched her nose for good measure.

Tip #17: Even with lots of pals to play with, some pets prefer humans.

While Big Wuzzy was occasionally ruining the stale air in our house and climbing into our cupboards, and Sox was chasing after Beanies and Rocky after plants, Chunky would play with any nearby ferret for a few minutes before following Mark or me around the house. Try as we had to get him one buddy after another, he continued to prefer our company.

Sweet and friendly as Chunky was, even he was a thief. In fact, having four ferrets in the house meant we couldn't leave boots or shoes on the floor without expecting to retrieve them from behind the TV, couch, and other furniture. Anything new—a box, purse, bag, anything—was an immediate target of curiosity and the contents in jeopardy of disappearing.

At times, this ferret pilfering was truly entertaining, such as when my mother sat watching her purse being raided, her keys dragged off, and her eyeglasses retreating and finally disappearing behind our couch. When I returned one of her tubes of lipstick half chewed and punctured, she threw it in the trash and said that ferrets weren't her favorite animals. I told her if she wasn't so materialistic she wouldn't mind ferrets quite so much. She pinched her nose in response.

In fact, ferrets aren't for everybody. In addition to people like my mom, ferrets aren't good pets for children because ferrets are unpredictable and fragile. In addition, ferrets aren't for people who don't like to look down, or people with girths so large they can't see their own feet, let alone a tiny ferret.

Ferrets also aren't right for lazy people because ferrets are a lot of work. And they're not usually good for college students because it's hard to control what other college students do—like open up the ferret cage as a joke or forget the ferret is running around. All the time ferrets roam around our house—a half-hour in the morning and at least an hour in the evening—we are constantly on the lookout for things that would get them into trouble. We'd heard many stories of people who'd had to have their ferret operated on because it ate something it shouldn't have (erasers being a favorite), who lost their ferret "somewhere in an apartment building" after the ferret climbed into a cupboard and went out an oversized hole meant only to accommodate the sink drain pipe, or whose ferret climbed up something high (like the side of its cage) and when it couldn't climb down, jumped down and injured itself. We didn't want to add to the stories.

Careful as we were, though, Rocky sneaked downstairs when Somebody forgot to shut the basement door. Our basement is dangerous because of the $17,000 in fishing tackle strewn about down there like random thoughts. Rocky also climbed up Big Wuzzy's cupboard and appeared on top of the stove one day while the stove was on. Another time, he clawed open the cupboard under the kitchen sink and climbed into the empty space between the outside of the dishwasher and the counter space that holds the dishwasher in place. It was because of Rocky that we finally put child-proof latches on our cupboard doors.

In addition to our needing to be careful, having ferrets also meant additional work around the house to keep one step ahead of hairballs, which, as with cats, can be a disgusting problem for little ferrets. Hairball prevention involved weekly laundering to de-hair the cut-off sweatshirts, sweatpants, fleece tops, towels, hammocks, and snuggy sacks the ferrets slept in and that kept them from falling very far in their cages. It also involved vacuuming, which is an underrated sport that people just plain don't get rewarded enough to do. Just once, I'd like to see a person with a vacuum cleaner on the front of a Wheaties box.

Spoiling ferrets requires even more work. Mark and I began each day by sharing our bagel bits with our pals, and letting them romp around the house before we departed for work. We left jeans on the floor so they could run up and down the legs, and we spread towels and sheets over boxes and overturned dog beds to make sure our boys had plenty of new things to amuse themselves with. Because the ferrets liked fresh water but couldn't handle it as neatly as we would have preferred, we draped a towel over the bathtub and put a bowl of water in the bottom, which they drank from and tipped over.

We also found ways to spoil each ferret individually. Sox got to pounce on balloons left over from the kids' birthday parties. He loved watching balloons rise into the air, jumping at them, and popping them. Of course, we had to pick up the bits immediately so he wouldn't eat them.

In the winter, Big Wuzzy loved to go outside and burrow in the snow with his leash and harness on. And when we didn't have enough snow to burrow in, I sometimes filled up a Coleman cooler with snow so he could burrow around. Big Wuzzy also liked to stick his face in a deeper bowl of water. More than once I took a large mixing bowl and filled it with water so he could stick his head in and look around underwater as if bobbing for apples.

Chunky was spoiled with a special tour of the heater ducts.

I had just completed a once-every-five-year vacuuming of each of the furnace-register vents, thought I had put all the vents back, and let the ferrets out to play. I was running after a pencil being dragged backward toward our leather couch when I saw a register cover on the carpet and a rectangular gaping hole nearby. My heart raced in my chest as I ran around and grabbed Rocky and the pencil he'd been dragging, removed Big Wuzzy from the cupboard and grabbed Sox running across the floor. As I ran to the cage to tuck the three ferrets away, I looked around for Chunky and called for him.

Trying not to panic, I knelt down next to the register vent. My heart stopped when I heard the pitter-patter of Chunky's little feet running down the vent that went to the furnace! I ran downstairs and started yelling, "NO, Chunky! Turn around, Chunky!" as if he could understand me. The pitter-patter, pitter-patter of his little feet got closer and closer to the furnace. I yelled "NO!" again as if it mattered. I imagined trying to rip the duct-work off the ceiling, yet knew I couldn't do anything in time to help Chunky.

The pitter-patter stopped. I held my breath. My heart stopped a second time. Suddenly, the pitter-patter started up again, only going in the opposite direction, back toward the living room. I ran upstairs and called quietly to Chunky so I wouldn't scare him. I waited for what seemed like minutes, quietly cheering him on. Suddenly, Chunky appeared, dust all over his little body, his little eyes peering up at me as if to say, "Wow, that was weird."

I picked him up, brushed him off, looked him over to make sure he hadn't hurt himself, gave him a big hug, and offered to let him bite me for being so careless. Instead, he licked my face.

The fact that Chunky licked my face was either because he needed salt or because ferrets, like dogs, know a little something about affection. Few people in the 1990s believed ferrets were capable of human-like emotion. In fact, because we'd heard stories of ferrets that had been euthanized after inadvertently biting somebody, we kept our ferrets from interacting with everyone who stopped over. The people that interacted with our ferrets were the trusted people we called upon to watch our pets when we went on vacation: Rick and Rick, Jr., one of my former supervisors and his son; Sylvia, a co-worker who had studied mink and saw some similarities to our ferrets; and our neighbors, Melissa and Pam.

In fact, if there is a godsend in this story, it's Melissa, who, with her mother, Pam, was counted on many a time to take care of our ferrets when we went on vacation. With our little guys under their care, I never worried that we'd come back from vacation and get handed a headless ferret because it had bitten one of its caregivers. Or handed a ferret pelt with the words, "Sorry, it just didn't work out." In fact, all Melissa and Pam ever left us were four happy ferrets. And a Glade air freshener. They must have seen my mom pinching her nose.

Tip #18: Saying good-bye to a pet is much harder than saying hello.

By the third year of my marriage, Sonic the Hedgehog had developed a bizarre neurological disease, and rather than watch her spend the rest of her life literally spinning around in circles—or, as Mark put it, charging people to watch Sonic break-dance on a plate—I took her to the veterinarian for a send-off to Hedgehog Heaven. I got this role because Mark was still teaching at the local community college to pay off Chunky's vet bills.

Taking Sonic to the Haslett Animal Hospital was hard, not only because our time with Mamma Hedgehog had come to an end, but because lying on her side in a box between bouts of spins, she looked like any other hedgehog. To make matters worse, a woman who came in with her pit bull peered into the box and said, "Oh, she's really cute."

I mumbled something like, "Thanks, but she's very ill," to justify to the stranger what I was doing. Of course, then I questioned what I was doing. As I contemplated taking Sonic home to continue her suffering into death, she looked at me with her sad charcoal eyes and I felt I'd made the right decision. A second later, I interpreted that same sad look to mean that she didn't like people staring at her, and that perhaps mine was a bad decision. Then the vet assistant was standing there asking me how she could help me and I could only say that I was the one who had called about the hedgehog.

Time passes slowly when an animal is being euthanized. As the guilt of choosing death over life swept over me, I wondered if I could have done something more for her like—I don't know—make the spinning less or turn the spinning into positive energy somehow, like converting it to light or something. I found myself unable to move away from the counter while I awaited the return of the assistant with the box and wondered what the lady with the pit bull thought of my killing the "cute" hedgehog, and wondered if I could pay the $18 for this service without getting pissed off, because, really, how much does it really cost the vet to put such a small animal to sleep?

I had lost all nerve and had turned to mush by the time the assistant handed me the box with Mamma Hedgehog's body. The assistant mumbled something about sending me a bill and that I should go home now and bury my little friend. I closed the top of the box, nodded, whispered thank you, and drove home to wait for Mark.

When Mark returned from work at 7:30 that spring evening, we dug a hole in our backyard between the dogs' kennel and the brush pile and deemed the area the Mamma Hedgehog Memorial Garden. Mark said a few words about how

Sonic was just the hedgehog he'd always wanted, was a good hedgehog, that he'd miss her, and he hoped we had done okay by her. I was out of energy and could only mumble, "God bless little Sonic." The next day, I placed a concrete hedgehog that we'd found at a local nursery on her grave.

Louie, meanwhile, who had been anything but interactive with us, found himself at a better home with two little girls who had stopped by because they understood we had a petting zoo. Last we heard, Louie was enjoying life in a home with those two little girls. Actually, the last I heard was from my sister, Aby, who let me know quite clearly she was miffed that I had given Louie away, then went on for several minutes about the terrible home she'd gone into to get him in East St. Louis, the scary drive because she thought he had died. She went on for so long, I was able to set the phone down and start a load of laundry.

With the hedgehogs gone and only the ferrets to tend to, Mark took an inventory of cages and aquariums under our deck and announced that we had numerous ones that were "ready for other creatures." With four children coming and going every other weekend, most holidays and a month in the summer, I was thinking four ferrets were enough to take care of. But I also knew something else was out there that Mark had always wanted. I just didn't know what that something was.

Tip #19: Some pesky pet pursuers are more persistent than others.

CHAPTER 4

Barking Up Another Tree

In my spare time, I sometimes wonder about all the forces that go into making certain events unfold. See, when I first met Mark, he had a German Shepherd the size of a miniature horse, so I assumed that if we ever got a dog, we'd end up with a giant canine that could knock me over with an energetic whip of its tail. Instead, in 1998, Mark happened to be in a pet store with Conrad and Elizabeth falling in love with a tiny white lhasa-bijon puppy. The fact that Mark fell for a small, pure white, non-hunting, frou-frou dog is pretty amazing. That a puppy came into my life at the point Mark thought we needed one is right up there with miraculous.

Mark met our future companion during one of those court-allotted Wednesday evenings with Conrad and Elizabeth. After feeding Conrad and Elizabeth at a restaurant near their suburban Detroit home, the threesome often found themselves in a mall and, eventually, a pet store. Their favorite pet store contained tiny rooms where people could play with puppies. Mark claims he and the kids had gone to this particular pet store numerous times, had played with several puppies, and that on the certain fateful evening as he was leaving the store, he saw the little white frou-frou puppy clawing at the corner of his cage. Mark claims the puppy did this "to get my attention," and that, "It was love at first sight." But he couldn't just bring the puppy home— he was on his way out the door to get the kids back to his Ex at the designated time, *and* he had a larger force to reckon with at home.

See, being practical, Germanic, hard-shelled, tightly wrapped and suffering with a sinus infection, I was happy with the critters we had and immediately said, "Thanks, but no."

Now, I think my answer should have sufficed. But no. "The Little White Puppy" was all Mark talked about, it was all Mark wanted, it was all he'd need for a very long time, AND it was everything I needed to improve my life. It was all I could do to keep from going bonkers. To end the blathering noise, I agreed the next night to drive back to the pet store—an hour away—to look at this great puppy. We did, and, amazingly, as Mark walked by, the little white puppy clawed crazily at the corner of the cage as if to get Mark's attention. Mark guided me into a tiny room, bursting with happiness when one of the blonde, cheerful clerks handed him the puppy. Mark snuggled the puppy, told him, "I hope we can take you home, little fella," and put him on the floor. The puppy wobbled up to me, sniffed at my shoes, then bit into a small squeaky toy and shook the crap out of the toy as if to kill it. As Mark went on about the puppy and how much fun it would be, my thoughts were: *It's out of control, it'll ruin things, it has too much energy, it will make messes, Mark won't clean up the poop—.* I shook my head and said simply, "I can live without him."

Mark whined and whimpered like a beaten dog all the way home. I was only grateful it wasn't warm enough for the car windows to be down, so other people wouldn't have to wonder what was making my husband suffer so. I looked over at a passing car and mouthed "HELP" to the passenger.

Later, over dinner, I mentioned that perhaps we could go for a walk at a natural area the next day. Mark said "Sure, but it'd be so much more fun with a puppy, don't you think?" Later, I mentioned that I had to be out of town for work two nights the next week. Mark said, "I'd be much less lonely if I had a puppy around." He then went on to mention several other reasons why a puppy was just what we needed. My favorite was, "If I'm ignoring you or not really listening to you, you'll always be able to talk to the puppy."

"And I can talk about you to the puppy when I'm out there cleaning up the dog poop," I said.

"I'll clean up the dog poop."

"And walk him every day and take him to obedience school and get his shots and—?"

"My, we are looking at the positive part of this, aren't we?" He signed.

"It's a big obligation and not to be taken lightly."

"Apparently not. I mean, of course not. And I'll do whatever's needed to take care of him." He paused and blinked at me with his puppy-dog eyes. "So, can we go get him tomorrow?"

It was enough to make a semi-sane person crazy. "If the puppy is at the store tomorrow, we'll bring him home."

The moment the store opened the next day, Mark called and asked about the puppy. He seemed to hold his breath until suddenly he exploded with, "Phew! I'm so relieved!" He told them we would come pick him up after work, and would they take our credit card number to hold it?

I couldn't get to pet store fast enough to get the puppy, to end the yappity-yap about the puppy and what life would be like with the puppy, and how the puppy would be my best and loyal friend. Mark nearly sprinted into the store, ran right up to the cage the little white puppy was in and announced, "We're taking you home!" In case the puppy needed any encouragement, Mark quickly moved his hands up and down to mimic the puppy's spastic clawing at the corner of the cage.

What a hit Mark was at the store, blabbing on about the cute puppy to the two cute clerks, who also were downright bubbly about the little white puppy. They told us how lucky we must feel, and how lucky for the puppy, and what a good pal he would be for us. It was as if they'd been coached by Mark in advance of my arrival. Or, they were flirting with Mark. Grrr.

I was unmoved and did not crack a smile while Mark filled out a bunch of paperwork and paid for the puppy. And I did not comment when the flirty pet store clerks put a goofy little blue bow on the puppy's head and brushed him until he looked like a big bag of cotton. Then the puppy was in my arms. One look into his scared little eyes and my heart jumped to my throat, my eyes got all watery, and my crusty outer shell melted away like drippy popcorn butter. I patted the puppy on the head and reassured him with, "Don't worry. We'll take good care of you."

On the way home, the puppy sat on Mark's lap, shivering and shaking. I wondered out loud if the puppy had a cold. Soon, he was frothing at the mouth, and I wondered if the little fella was rabid. In answer to my question, the puppy made this gag reflex sound and, in a flash, a small pile of nice warm barf appeared on the floor of my car.

"Oh, how cute," Mark smiled. "He has motion sickness."

"Barf is not cute, no matter how cute the animal it comes from."

"I see your attitude hasn't changed at all," Mark grumped.

"I see yours hasn't, either, Mister I-Got-My-Puppy. What's his name anyway?"

"Dusty."

At home, we took a half a billion photos of Dusty in the grass, first with the goofy bow, then without it. He was a bit wobbly from the ride, a bit frothy at the mouth, and his eyes a bit far away, as if the world was still spinning and he wasn't quite sure where he'd landed. I felt sorry for him: uprooted from a puppy farm and his mom and siblings, shipped off to a store, stuck in a cage for who knows how long, and played with by several strangers, many of whom probably thought he was out of control and perhaps too expensive. Then he was combed and fluffed, and driven in a car that made him sick, to a strange place with a strange man and a formerly normal woman.

I scooped the little fella up, carried him inside, and set about making a nest for him in a small, oval-shaped bed we'd picked up along with 20 tons of dog food and treats on the way home. I lined the bed with a dozen of Mark's and my shirts to remind the puppy that he was stuck with us no matter. Perhaps too tired from his long day, Dusty slept the night without a sound.

> Tip #20: When a man (or child) promises to take care of the critter they want, don't believe them.

Indeed, Dusty was all any obsessed person would ever need to take their mind off anything else that ailed them. Immediately, I was all about Dusty—checking on him in the morning, guiding his little puppy self outside to pee, watching over him from inside the house so that no wandering bad dog or roaming pterodactyl would come and take him away. After work, Dusty was the first animal to be attended to—rushed outside as if his bladder was going to burst, coached and encouraged, his every poop and pee celebrated. Inside, we played with him, selecting from what soon became a small mountain of toys and bones. We took him for walks, snuggled him, and tucked him in his bed at night. For the first several months, it seemed it really was all about Dusty.

Unfortunately for me, part of being all about Dusty was taking him to a vet for vaccinations, an event I really wanted nothing to do with. See, shots involve sharp, pointy things that smell bad and hurt worse, and I have been known to pass out when such items are poked in my arm. Watching other people—or animals for that matter—endure shots is also something I avoid whenever possible.

But was I going to tell that to Mark? No. I simply told him that he had promised to take the lead on all things Dusty and that he had to go.

"You mean by myself?"

"I think you can handle it."

"But, we're partners and pals," he frowned.

"And you can handle it without me."

Pause. Blink, blink of his puppy-dog eyes.

"Okay," I caved. "I'll make the appointment, you hold the dog on the table."

"Why?"

"That's the deal, or I don't go."

"You don't like shots even for dogs?"

I offered my best frowny face and made the appointment, never guessing then that Mark would turn out to be the more vulnerable in front of the vet.

On the five-minute drive to the vet, Dusty frothed at the mouth and gave all appearances that he was going to barf on the floor again. When he didn't barf, I thought perhaps the rest of the visit would go off without a hitch. Immediately inside the door of the animal hospital, however, Dusty started whining and shaking violently. Mark and I sat down on a bench and Dusty tried to launch himself from the slippery floor onto Mark's lap, then mine. He made this muffled yowling noise when a clerk took him to get weighed. In a private room a few minutes later, Dusty whined, shook and yelped. To top it all off, he peed on the floor when the vet entered the room.

The vet was a guy and he had a name and everything, but he wasn't too memorable because, well, I wasn't exactly plugged in and paying attention. I was too busy worrying about the impending shots. The nameless male vet asked questions about how Dusty was acting, how he was eating, whether he was doing anything abnormal, whether we had brought a stool sample. I loved the last question, because Mark—the consummate biologist—warned me in advance that he refused to pay anyone to analyze any poop from any of our animals. His responses varied, but usually were something colorful like, "I have a microscope and can't think of anything better to do later except check out all my ferrets' poop." On this visit his answer was, "I'll check it out under a microscope and call you if I find anything that's wiggling."

The vet's eyes rolled from Mark to my blank stare, to the door. As he mumbled something about going to get the vaccinations, Mark suddenly morphed from the confident Scat Man to saying, "Uh, I just want to ask you something."

The vet turned, perhaps fearful that the question had to do with analyzing dog scat, and was almost relieved when

Mark pointed shyly at Dusty's stomach and said, "I just want to make sure he's okay and everything. But I've never seen spots like that on a puppy's tummy."

The vet smiled, and after assuring Mark that Dusty's dark pigmented smears against an otherwise pink tummy were perfectly normal, shot me this perplexed look as if he didn't quite know what to make of my husband.

I shrugged.

Mark said, "Phew! I was worried."

After the vet left to get Dusty's shots, I was about to ask whether any of the famous basset hound puppies Mark's parents raised had little splotches on their tummies when Mark said, "Dusty is such a special puppy. Feel this."

"Feel what?" I asked, not wanting to feel anything. I knew the shots were on their way and being numb seemed perfectly appropriate. Besides, this was hardly the time for me to be standing up.

"Just come here for a moment."

I stood warily. Mark took my hand and guided it to Dusty's shoulder.

"He has shoulders," I said, taking my hands away and sitting down.

"You didn't feel his wing nubbins?" Mark asked. "That's where his angel wings used to be before they fell off and he came down here to be with us. He's Dusty, the Angel Pup."

It was too much. I didn't know which was cuter: Mark or Dusty. All I could do was shake my head and smile and wonder how in the world this puppy had completely and totally enthralled my husband. And how quickly Dusty had won me over as well.

Truly, Dusty is a special dog. If he doesn't melt your heart with the simple look of his chocolate brown eyes set against pure white wavy hair, he'll get you when he begs for attention by sitting on his hind legs and waving his front paws up and down. If his heart-melting eyes, begging and tail wagging don't get you, then his happy jaunt as he carries his favorite stuffed animal to the door before going outside will surely do the trick. And if that doesn't do it, then surely his loyalty will.

The loyal Lhasa Apso part of Dusty came from the guard dogs and companions of the Tibetan monasteries, an origin traceable, well, not as far back as the dinosaurs perhaps, but a long time ago. The American Kennel Club states that the character of the Lhasa Apso is: *Gay and assertive, but chary of strangers.*

For the record, Dusty is not gay as our gay-lesbian-leary society would think of it. He is not, for example, running around humping other male dogs, having his nails done and wearing poofy clothes. Dusty is the old-fashioned gay, as in merry.

While "chary" isn't a word I use every day, Mark's 1951 printing of *The American College Dictionary* says that it means "careful; wary." Dusty is very wary and chary. And merry. His modus operandi in the wee hours of the morning is to run out the front door full speed to the end of his rope to bark at any person or dog foolish enough to venture by. His duty continues inside by picking up a toy and sitting guard in the entrance to the bathroom until Mark and I are ready for work. It's a great quality if you ask me: guarding two people doing their business in the bathroom while resting one's fuzzy face on a cute stuffed animal. It's all the makings of a Norman Rockwell painting, less the dripping faucet in the bathtub and the gold tile on the wall.

After work, Dusty runs outside to guard us from the evils lurking in the front yard, and returns to spend a few hours near the kitchen making sure that things like steaks and desserts don't suddenly start wiggling and moving around in the kitchen on their own. The rest of Dusty's evening is spent somewhere on the floor close to me, gnawing on a rawhide or otherwise watching my every keystroke as I work on the computer. When I announce it's time for a walk, he drops whatever he's doing, runs up to me and patiently waits while I get myself ready. While we walk, he is constantly leery, always watching, sometimes to the point of being downright aggravating; when he thinks some noise or some passing person is a potential threat, he locks his legs, puffs out his barrel chest and refuses to move until the perceived threat is gone. Trying to move him when he's locked in a defensive position is as easy as moving an overweight mule.

The Bichon Frise part of Dusty is the impractical, happy, leaping dog that makes us laugh. The official Web site for The Bichon Frise Club of America, Inc. states:

> *The Bichon Frise is a small, sturdy, white powder puff of a dog whose merry temperament is evidenced by his plumed tail carried jauntily over the back and his dark-eyed inquisitive expression.*

According to the Bichon Frise Club of America, the temperament of the bijon frise is:

> *Gentle mannered, sensitive, playful and affectionate. A cheerful attitude is the hallmark of the breed and one should settle for nothing less.*

Dusty is so sensitive to being scolded that his curly fur actually flattens out on top of his head when Mark raises his voice. And if a "cheerful attitude is the hallmark of the breed," take the summer of 2004, when Dusty went with me to a local pet store, walked right up to a bin of stuffed squeaky toys, selected a bright orange spider with long dangly legs, picked it up gently in his mouth and carried it past the cashier and right out the door. It doesn't get any more cheerful than that.

Dusty was just the playful pal Mark had hoped for. As a puppy, he fetched squeaky plush toys, flung bones into the air before chewing on them, and chased toys that Mark dragged around himself in a circle. If Dusty got frustrated during that game of keep-away, he'd bark, launch himself at Mark, and work himself into a near frenzy. At his most ferocious, Dusty looked like a rabid dog launching himself at his prey. In response, Mark had to either cover himself with a blanket so Dusty couldn't get to him, or cover Dusty up with a blanket and tell him to settle down. If Mark stopped playing too soon, Dusty would drop the plush toy on Mark's lap and push down on the toy with his nose to make the toy squeak.

One year, Mark put a fuzzy stuffed chicken in Conrad's Easter basket and Dusty stole it and bit into it, causing the rooster to "cock-a-doodle-doo!" The crowing noise caused Dusty to bark, growl and bite the rooster again, making it "cock-a-doodle-doo!" again, which made Dusty bark and growl even more. This vicious cycle continued until Mark had to take the toy away. Dusty's favorite toys are the ones that imitate real animals, my favorite of which is a screaming howler monkey.

Dusty also became the Burrow Dog when he spontaneously burrowed and snuggled his way under pillows, towels, blankets and laundry, his fuzzy head and charcoal eyes popping out from under the other end of the pile. When he barked inside the pile or came out the other end, it was an invitation to tackle him gently, whereupon he nibbled at us through the cloth.

When he just stayed under the pile with his head sticking out, it was simply the cutest sight in the world.

Loyal, cute, and fun as Dusty was as a puppy, however, nothing could make up for the horrible hormones that took over his body when he was six months old. One day, he became rudely amorous with the leg of a friend who was sitting at our kitchen table sipping coffee. I suggested to Mark that perhaps we should get Dusty castrated. Truly, I underestimated the power of such a word to a guy who loves his male dog, because I was hushed into silence, scolded for being a male-hater and all sorts of other ridiculous things.

A week later, another friend stopped by and suffered the same personal attentions from Dusty. When that friend—a male—suggested, "That damn dog needs its balls whacked off," Mark looked visibly hurt. But after his buddy went home, Mark conceded to "neutering, not castration" (even though they're the same), and only after making a call to a local veterinarian. The conversation went something like this:

"Yes, I understand you might be able to preserve some of my dog's sperm?"

My eyebrows nearly shot off the top of my head.

"It's how much?" he sighed. "Okay, thank you."

Before I could figure out how to respond to the question, Mark was sharing the answer. "It costs a thousand dollars."

I nodded. "I'm sorry . . . I think. I mean, you're not going to—."

"I was just thinking how cool it would be is all. I know we can't afford it. Poor Dusty."

Tip #21: Some men take the neutering of their dog personally.

It was bad enough that our brave guard dog turns instantly into a shivering, cowering puffball just stepping foot inside the animal hospital. But this particular visit to the vet was for something much more long-term than the simple prick of a nasty needle. Now, Dusty didn't know that he was being dropped off and would awaken later missing a couple of parts, but Mark knew. In fact, Mark rambled on about, "Poor Dusty. He didn't mean to hump. He's not a bad boy. Amy, are you sure we have to? You're such a meany." When I didn't respond, he turned his attention to Dusty and explained, "Mean Mom is taking you to get your nuts chopped off."

During the five minutes we waited to see the vet, I suffered horribly. Dusty shivered and shook and whined as Mark told him he should fondle his nuts one more time before he lost them. As Mark told him to kiss his manhood good-bye, and reminded him once again that he would never have a shot at being a Dad Dog, Dusty howled. Then Dusty peed on the floor. I was never so happy to see a vet in all my life.

Dusty recovered within days and sprang back to become a full-fledged puppy, bouncing with exuberance and demanding every last minute of Mark's and my attention. We played with him, ran with him, wrestled with him, bought him toys, bought him bones, talked to him. Still, it wasn't enough. The little energetic puppy was simply driving us both nuts.

The solution, Mark said, was another dog.

Shortly thereafter, via another bizarre alignment of the moon with a planet, asteroid or hemorrhoid, I found myself back at the pet store Dusty came from, looking at puppies. This time, it was going to be my puppy, Mark said, and I got to pick out any one I wanted as long it was a lhasa-bijon mix.

My problem was that there were three lhasa-bijon mixes and I wanted all three of them. In fact, once I realized I could take one puppy home, I turned into absolute mush and suddenly wanted to take the Shih-Tzu, and the Pomeranian and the one next to it, and, well, maybe not that skinny, yippy thing, but most of the animals, because I could give them a great home. Choose one? How cruel. And what if the two that looked similar were sisters or brothers? I didn't want to separate them—take one home and leave the other for some potentially mean home? It was too much.

While I was suffering from surreal duress, I supposedly told Mark that I wanted a lapdog that would lick my face. I played with two lhasa-bijon mixes, was licked by one, and Mark said that since that matched my criteria we should take her home. All the way home I wanted the other one that looked like the one I had on my lap only bigger. And I told Mark. And he almost went back to get the other one, too. So I told him I was kidding. But I wasn't. I wanted both of them. All three of them. Most of them.

The puppy I brought home was caramel brown with a face that looked like it had been dipped in black paint. I named her Little Dipper. While Dusty had a classic Bichon Frise bent tail, Little Dipper had a cropped tail that never wagged back and forth correctly. In fact, it was the first dog tail I ever saw that sometimes wagged from left to center and back again without going to the other side. She maxed out at 15 pounds, which was about half Dusty's weight, and had teeth orthodontists dream about. Her Lhasa-Apso-derived trait of watchdog was evident only in the car when Dusty's delicate stomach prevented him from fulfilling his usual duties.

Little Dipper expressed her Bichon Frise genes by leaping up and down repeatedly every time I took her leash off the pantry doorknob. She also napped under stacks of pillows, licked any hapless person that sat on one of our chairs, and was the huntress of the family. Once, she chased a deer three-quarters of a mile before I could catch up to her and threaten to mush her cute, fuzzy little face into the dirt.

Dusty and Little Dipper hit it off instantly. And because they did, and with Dipper being a female and all, and the dogs being so cute and all, "Well," said Mark, "Why don't we breed Little Dipper?"

The very idea of Dipper having puppies was stressful for me, because our local vet suggested that Dipper's head was large in comparison to the rest of her body, meaning a C-section would be most likely required if she did have puppies. After Mark poo-pooed that thought, he listed a dozen reasons why we should have puppies, including that I had never experienced puppies being born. To that, I countered that I had also never had to give puppies away and the very idea of doing that was enough to send me twitching and cowering into a corner. Me, give away cute puppies to strangers? Me, separate Dipper from her offspring? Are you kidding?

I then added the logical thought that perhaps there were already enough cute puppies in the world. Mark countered with, "Yeah, but my parents paid for trips to Florida each year as a result of selling our basset hound puppies," to which I responded with, "Goody gumdrops for them. They were evil people and hated their own puppies. So nerts to that."

About once a year for the next six years, Mark brought up the idea of Dipper having puppies, and each year Dipper went without having any puppies or, for that matter, getting spayed. Of course not being spayed meant that every six months or so, Dipper was a hot commodity, and Dusty was in love. He followed Dipper around the house with his face inches from her rear-end, panting happily wherever she went. He'd mount her again and again, and they'd mate inside or outside. Privately or with an audience. It was a happy time for Dusty.

Well, at least most of this love time was happy. See, dogs have this lock-on device that essentially locks the dogs together to prevent another male from mating with the female. After some of their sexual romps, Dusty and Dipper would get stuck together—end to end—for up to twenty minutes. I remember well the Saturday morning I looked outside to check on the dogs in broad daylight, found them stuck together where all the passing world could see them. I imagined a young mother walking along with her kid in a stroller, the kid pointing to my dogs and asking, "Mommy, why are the dogs stuck together like that?"

I called to Mark, and after we counted to three, he gently picked Dusty up while I picked Dipper up, and, carefully as we could, we carried our two stuck dogs inside the house.

In exchange for gaining a sex partner and girlfriend, Dusty had to share his food dish, his water bowl, his fuzzy toys, and often, his bones. Even though I always gave each dog their own rawhide bones, for some reason one of the two bones was always the envy of both dogs. For whatever reason, a partially chewed rawhide bone—chewed to the point of being soft and flexible—was something to whine about and required parental interference.

At first, Dipper seemed to have the upper paw in claiming the sought-after, broken in bone. She'd come out of the bedroom in the morning or come in from outside, and sprint to wherever the partially chewed, coveted bone last was. Dusty would follow, lie next to her and whine now and again as he watched the bone disappear. If I handed him the other, less chewed bone, he'd ignore it and let it fall to the floor untouched until he was convinced the coveted soft one was gone.

Not to be outsmarted for long, however, Dusty began taking the coveted bone outside with him, or hid it in his bed or behind the TV. While Dipper eventually sniffed out any bone in his bed or behind the TV, taking the bone outside with him allowed Dusty to keep his eye on the bone and increased his likelihood of being able to continue chewing on the bone after he carried it back inside.

The dogs also got their own oval-shaped wicker beds with soft, comfy pads. Their beds were placed in a hallway-alcove where the three bedrooms and a bathroom came together. Separating this hallway-alcove from the rest of the house was a door, making it such that any Boogie Man that attempted to sneak through the first door would have to take on a combined weight of 45 pounds of ankle-biting canine before they could get to Mark and me.

Ferocious as they might be toward the Boogie Man, both dogs got along well with the ferrets. Funny thing, though: A ferret sees a small, fuzzy dog as nothing more than a large stuffed toy to drag off and tuck away behind a piece of furniture. In fact, when Dusty was just a puppy, Rocky grabbed Dusty by the neck and tried to pull him behind the green La-Z-Boy chair. A few weeks later, Dusty was large enough to pick Rocky up by the neck and drag him off. I grabbed both Dusty and Rocky by the scruff of their necks, called a truce and from that point, no scruffing or dragging occurred between the two. Instead, Rocky occasionally grabbed onto Dusty's chest and hung on while Dusty walked him slowly around the house.

Little Dipper ignored the ferrets except when we fed them bits of Pop-Tart, raisins or cereal. Then she'd hang around and eat the bits of food they left on the ground. When the food was put away and the floor was clean, Little Dipper ignored the ferrets once again.

Life with two dogs and four ferrets fell into a regular pattern. The morning routine consisted of letting the dogs out and back in first thing, letting the ferrets out to play and eat treats, and tucking them back in their cage before going to work. Upon our return home, the process was repeated. Between sporadic and unfocused bouts of other activity, we did ferret laundry, took the dogs on excursions to a pet store for dog toys, trimmed the dogs' fur with scissors, trimmed ferret toe nails, and vacuumed ferrets when they excavated a bean bag chair and all the teeny bits of Styrofoam stuck to their little fur. The dogs got nearly daily walks, and at least once a week, a long romp at a local park or wildlife area. I took plastic bags with me to clean up poop and only once so far have I reached into the pocket of my jacket the morning after a walk to find an unpleasant brown something oozing out of a plastic bag.

And speaking of poop, as I predicted, Mark has never lifted a spade—or finger—to pick up dog poop. One might say that for his promises, I fell poop, line and stinker.

Tip #22: If people get to go on vacation, it only stands to reason that dogs should, too.

Like most dog owners, we took our dogs on "Pups Vacations," which were overnight camping trips to Lake Michigan so that Dipper could run like the wind, chase any shorebird she saw, and swim out into the waves to try to jump on my air mattress with me. Meanwhile, Dusty would run like the barrel-chested heavyweight he is, moving mightily for 100 feet perhaps, before walking out into the waves for a drink and a swim. After rolling on a dead fish, he'd dig down an inch into the sand and lie down. Dipper would eventually join us, dropping a bunch of wet sand on our lap as she sat her wiggly self down.

Before leaving for the evening, we'd entice the dogs into Lake Michigan one more time to try to rinse off the fish smell, the sand and anything else they'd found to roll in. Afterward, it was usually cool enough that Mark and I felt comfortable leaving the dogs in the car while we ate at our favorite local Mexican restaurant for dinner. That, of course, gave the dogs plenty of time to roll around the towel-lined car and make it stinky, sandy and wet. There's nothing like returning from the pleasant ambience of a quaint restaurant to the fishy, wet-dog smell of a car.

After dinner, we often stopped by an ice cream store that just happened to be on the way to the campground. Now, feeding a dog ice cream takes some practice. See, the first time we bought the dogs ice cream, we got cones. Dusty took one lick and his scoop of vanilla fell onto the grass. He ate it in two gulps, snarfed down the cone, then sat and stared as Little Dipper politely licked hers. When hers was gone, Dusty sat and stared at Mark and me. On every other Pups Vacation after that, we've gotten the pups ice cream in small dishes and held them between our feet so it takes longer for them to eat, and so that we can enjoy our ice cream without being stared at.

After ice cream, we'd head to camp and discuss who was going to fetch wood and who was going to keep the dogs from barking at passersby. The dogs, meanwhile, figured out amazing ways to wrap their long leashes around the picnic table, trees, and tent stakes, which made them all the more frustrated when a dog walked by. When they weren't making a tangled mess of themselves, they were digging holes, sniffing through leaves and doing just about everything a dog can do to help bring dirt into our tent.

At bedtime, the dogs would saunter right onto our sleeping bags. Dusty the Burrow Dog was amazing at heading right to the opening of a sleeping bag, rolling around and coming out pretty much dirt-free. Dipper, on the other hand, would search for the opening of the bag, go inside, curl up and attempt to go to sleep. There's nothing more inspirational for a good night's sleep than holding a sleeping bag upside down and watching dirt sprinkle out, only to have the dogs try to wiggle their wet, sandy selves back inside again.

We did lots of Pups Vacations over the years, my favorite of which went something like this:

We packed up the two dogs, the two youngest kids and a large aluminum canoe. I had a Cavalier with a rack on top to carry the big aluminum canoe, and Mark had our old Dodge conversion van to carry everything and everyone else. I was following Mark and enjoying some quiet music on the radio and all seemed to be going well, until an hour into the trip when Mark exited the highway without warning and pulled over to the far side of a gas station parking lot. Curious, I opened the side door of the van and was met with two kids wearing bandanas over their faces, trying to get out of the van. On the floor at their feet was a big pile of barf and, nearby, a small pile of poop. I put leashes on the two dogs and walked them in some grass nearby, laughing out loud. Behind me, Mark commanded the kids to clean up after the dogs. When they said, "I don't think so, Dad," I kept on walking and laughing.

Camping was fun, too. See, Dipper was only a few months old then, so we'd brought along a tiny dog cage that we set up inside the tent and lined with a half dozen towels and sweatshirts. Come time for bed, we all crawled into our sleeping bags, while Dusty found a spot between Mark's legs and Dipper settled into her cage. In the middle of the night, I awoke to a whimpering sound and saw Little Dipper clawing at the side of her cage. I picked her up and set her outside to let her pee. As I was zipping the tent back up, Little Dipper wobbled off across the mass of bodies and sleeping bags and disappeared. The flashlights were all on the other side of the tent with everyone else sleeping happily in between, so I patted the sleeping bags and crawled slowly toward the top of my sleeping bag. There, right inside the top of my bag, Little Dipper was all curled up. I picked her up, slid inside, and she curled up next to my shoulder. I felt her little sigh as she fell asleep. I meanwhile, did not sleep much at all because I was afraid I'd roll over and crush my young puppy.

The next day we went canoeing on the lower Platte River, which is a wide, winding river that empties into Lake Michigan. It was spring, during the kids' break, and only about 55 degrees. But we'd come to camp and canoe, and by golly, we were going to carry through with our plans. To heck with the chilly weather, we said, and to heck with the grayish clouds forming overhead. We had sweatshirts and cheesy rain gear and were ready for everything. Well, almost.

We'd just gotten everyone settled into the big aluminum canoe when Dusty walked to the starboard side and, with a mere second's hesitation, launched himself into the river. He sank like a stone up to his ears and his eyes grew big as he suddenly found himself paddling his big burly legs. The water was rather frothy as he circled quickly and came back to the canoe. I leaned over and pulled our very heavy, wet dog back into the canoe. Dusty thanked me by drenching me with the water he shook off his thick fur. Elizabeth grabbed a towel and wiped Dusty off. As soon as he was free, Dusty put his feet up on the gunwales as if ready to launch himself again. We spent the rest of the two-hour float trying to get Dusty to sit down.

Meanwhile, the temperature dropped another five degrees and the grayish clouds morphed into true rain clouds. We were within sight of the take-out spot near Lake Michigan when the sky opened up, dropping a chilling rain all over us. Little Dipper began shivering and whining, so we asked Elizabeth to open her spacious rain jacket and hold Dipper inside. Mark and I paddled furiously, got the boat to within five feet of the landing when Dusty launched himself into the water again. We pulled him back in, beached the boat, unloaded the dogs and kids, and got them all tucked away and whining in the car. Mark and I loaded up the canoe, accusing each other of the "great idea this was" and agreeing to "not do this again. Ever."

But of course, we did. Because we couldn't afford to take the kids on spring breaks and well, the word "camping" made both dogs run happily around in circles.

Tip #23: Dogs love camping at any time of year.

Being hearty and stupid outdoors people, we even took the pups winter camping. See, the beaches on Lake Michigan get these nifty little ice shelves that hang out over the water, often with ice-sand icicles hanging off them. It's quite a lovely place to walk around because the ice-sand formations are different every time. Dusty loves cold weather, and until he got older, subzero temperatures didn't keep him from wandering into Lake Michigan for a quick swim. Dipper took a frigid dip in Lake Michigan once and whined and moaned for an hour afterward as we toweled her off and kept her wrapped in warm blankets. She avoided the cold water after that.

The dogs also liked to see what dead things they could find on the beach in the winter. Dusty rolled in such lovelies and Dipper tried to remove them from the ice to get a better look, or perhaps a taste. One year, Dipper pulled on a frozen salmon so hard her two rear legs went into the air.

As soon as the sun would set below the winter horizon, we'd snuggle down in our tent. Mark and I got inside our zipped-together, down bags, and within seconds the dogs maneuvered for the best spot. Dusty headed for a spot between my legs on top of the bag, while Dipper assaulted my face for a lick and then moved quickly inside my bag. Mark must have smelled bad or something because they never seemed to migrate to him.

Being a dog sandwich and unable to move much during the night, I tended to wake up stiff as a board the next morning and craving aspirin. After a couple of winter trips in such a condition, I came up with the brilliant idea of bringing extra sleeping bags just for the dogs, the idea being that they would sleep in their own beds. I went to sleep with the dogs nearby and in their own sleeping bags, only to wake up with a dog between my legs and one inside my sleeping bag.

With the winter sun's rising, we'd eat at a local restaurant, feed the dogs the leftovers and return to the beach to play for a couple of hours. As with any other Pups Vacation, on the three-hour ride home, both dogs and Mark would sleep without stirring. I'm not sure how I became the primary driver on our Pups Vacations. Perhaps I just resigned myself to the fact that it's the least I could do given that Mark had described camping once as "An opportunity to ruin my back while sleeping on the hard ground just to make you and the dogs happy." Quite the sport, isn't he?

Tip #24: Some animals don't live as long as they should.

All in all, it wasn't a tough life being a dog in our house. Or a ferret for that matter. All the animals got along well enough, with Dusty playing with the ferrets and Dipper getting out of their way. A few years passed. Then another. Then one day, the weasel war dances declined, Big Wuzzy pounced less often, Rocky quit jumping into plants, Sox seemed to forget where his Beanie Babies were, and Chunky no longer begged for bagels, probably because they were too hard for his elderly teeth to chew. All four ferrets lost fur on their tails, which is an indication that their kidneys were failing. I could feel the ferreting years slipping away.

If there are two days an obsessed pet owner can describe clearly, it's the day they brought their pet home and the day the animal died. Chunky, the oldest, was suffering quietly with kidney problems, was hard of hearing and couldn't see well. In 2003, I worried about him every day of our 21-day vacation in Montana. When we returned, I was thrilled to find his wanton eyes staring at me. His gaze was far away, though, and it was as if he'd waited for us to return, because within hours of my tucking him away after one last romp on the floor, his breathing became quick and heavy. Within 48 hours of our return, Chunky had gone off to ferret heaven. I cried at the loss of my little friend, because Chunky had been simply the best ferret in the world.

We buried Chunky in the backyard with Sonic, in the area we called the Mama Hedgehog Memorial Garden. It's an area just outside the dog kennel and consists of several overgrown holly bushes, some other bushy thing and a small concrete hedgehog. As I covered Chunky's grave with a dozen small rocks that formed a "C," I thanked Chunky for sharing his life with us and for fighting with us when the vets had given up on him. And then I cried again.

Rocky suffered a series of seizures, each of which left him weak and his eyes far away for a day or so afterwards. After one particularly nasty seizure, he lost mobility of his back legs. To help him hobble around I got on my knees and scooted around on the floor while holding up his back legs. When I tired of that, Rocky just kept dragging himself by his front legs, as Chunky had after he'd broken his back.

During Rocky's slow and likely painful decline, the only true expression of his pain culminated in a wild scream when I returned home from work one day. He was blind, hardly able to get around, and since he was screaming in pain, we decided to put him down. It was the first ferret whose suffering we ended, because it was too much for us, or too much for him, or for all of us. Something like that anyway.

We buried Rocky with Sonic and Chunky in the Mama Hedgehog Memorial Garden. Mark told him he was a good ferret the last couple of years. I told him that he was a good ferret all of his years, less the thing he had with plants.

Sox died soon after. His was a brief funeral held inside the house because it was winter and very cold. Mark waited until after dark to bury Sox, because we didn't want the neighbors to see us bury the dead in the dead of winter. Mark did his best to bury Sox in the backyard sort of near Sonic and Chunky. But it was hard to dig a hole, and Mark later told me that he thought it'd be easier to dig near the house—okay right outside the back door. He didn't know then it was kind of a bad idea.

With Sox gone, that left Big Wuzzy to slowly wind down like a worn out clock. As with the others that preceded him, I tried to make him as comfortable as possible. I did extra laundry to make sure he had a clean place to snuggle, bought special mushy food when the hard crunchy stuff was a struggle for him to chew, and gave him little rub-downs in case he had some aches and pains. Big Wuzzy went from sleep to heaven tucked away in my favorite old sweatshirt.

What amazed me was that as each of the 1.5 pound fuzzy tube socks suffered in their own way—through kidney failure or seizures, hearing loss and blindness, and heaven knows what else—they did so without moaning, without groaning. Except for Rocky's single outburst, all four ferrets passed with quiet dignity.

By December 2003, the cage of ferrets was tucked away under our deck. The only ferret reminders were a few hammocks tucked in a drawer, a few photographs on the walls, and the bare patches of carpet in front of the bedroom doors. The remains of all four ferrets were buried in our yard, in the Mama Hedgehog Memorial Garden.

Well, mostly in the Mama Hedgehog Memorial Garden. And mostly buried. The following spring, while sitting in our hot tub, I noticed this tiny skull, shaped like a ferret's head, near the back door right next to the house. When I pointed it out to Mark he smiled sheepishly and said, "God rest the rest of Sox, then, huh."

I frowned and shook my head.

"I'll bury him properly now that I can dig a better hole," Mark said.

I smiled, patted him on the back and announced that, "If any of our other pets die in the winter, let's keep them in the freezer until conditions allow for a proper burial."

"Yes, we can wrap them in freezer paper and label them 'Dead pet. Do not eat.'"

Little did I know that one day we would have to do just that.

Tip #25: Most pets bought for children end up being cared for by the most responsible adult in the family.

Tip #26: Sometimes the person you *hope* will be the most responsible adult isn't.

CHAPTER 5

Of Mice, Gerbils and Pigs

One day right before the demise of the last of the ferrets, Mark and Elizabeth were shopping at Meijer, a local store, in search of some fish for the 100-gallon fish tank Mark had recently acquired from a friend. After looking over the fish, they wandered by a few other pets, and found themselves face to face with a small aquarium containing two adult guinea pigs. One was black and white with pink on its ears and the other was brown and white with brown ears. The small aquarium offered them little room to run around and squeal like, well, pigs, and at that moment, several things came together: Elizabeth's 13th birthday was approaching and we didn't have a present for her yet; Elizabeth expressed interest in rescuing the two guinea pigs; Mark had never had a guinea pig before; and they were on sale.

And so in February 2003, Pinky and Lincoln became Elizabeth's birthday presents and came to take up residence in our front entryway. Now, my knowledge of guinea pigs is:

1) that they might have come from New Guinea; 2) that South Americans raise them to eat; and 3) that they make this "wheek, wheek, wheek" sound that isn't very pig-like at all. I didn't know what they ate, the proper size for a cage, or what they did in their spare time. So, we put them in one of our numerous empty aquariums, covered the aquarium with several stacks of music albums in case the robust chubby things could figure out how to catapult out of the aquarium, and ran off to Soldan's to learn something about our new charges.

The staff at Soldan's know everything about pets and when we asked about what kind of cage to get they suggested one with a plastic bottom (for ease of cleaning), metal sides (in case the pigs chewed plastic?), and doors on the side and on top (for ease of access). Soldan's had a few cages that met these criteria, the largest of which was 38 inches long, 20 inches wide and 19 inches high. They also suggested Mardis Gras guinea pig food, a large, sturdy, ceramic bowl, a plastic hut, and a container to hold the ever-important timothy hay, said to keep the pigs' digestion just so. We added to our cart everything they suggested, plus two small and overly expensive bags of timothy hay, four little cubes of pressed alfalfa, a bag of recycled, pressed paper labeled "pet bedding" that allowed the manufacturer to charge $16 a bag, and some colored, munchy sticks to give the pigs something to gnaw on. All said, the inexpensive guinea pigs cost us about a hundred dollars to get up and running.

Now, Mark and I are not the type to measure before we buy things, and it was just a stroke of luck that the guinea pig cage fit perfectly on a structure inside our front door that looks like a small counter-nooky thing. Rising three feet off the ground, the counter previously held artificial plants that I hated because they did nothing but sit around and gather dust. Not being the type to dust except when VIPs gave ample warning of their impending arrival, I was quite happy to pluck the dusty, fake plants from their green Styrofoam, toss the plants and foam away, cover the counter with a big slab of particle board and place the new cage on top.

The first step toward getting the pigs settled involved lining the cage with recycled paper bedding. Elizabeth made a giant slit in the side of one of the plastic bags, turned it upside down and pulled out half of the bag's contents. As I was helping her spread the bedding around the bottom of the cage, I did some quick math: if the pigs' bedding had to be changed once a week, that's four times a month, at $8 for ½ a bag; that equals $32/month x 12 months = $384/year in bedding.

OMG.

They better be really nice pigs.

On top of the bedding we placed the plastic hut and the sturdy, ceramic dish purchased for their special Mardis Gras guinea pig food. Elizabeth filled up the bowl with food and attached two water bottles to the front of the cage, while I hung up a plastic tray that allowed the pigs to extract timothy hay any time of the day or night. As I added some of the timothy to the tray, I couldn't help but think that it looked like timothy grass I'd seen growing in the wild, which was followed by the thought that timothy for pigs in a small bag for $6 was a rip-off. And let's see, if the pigs went through a bag of timothy every other week, that's $12 a month times 12 months or $144 a year.

OMG.

Months later, we would wander around the local wildlife area and pluck our own timothy grass, which saved us a lot of money but resulted in Mark getting stung by a bee. Soon after, a co-worker who raises horses, pigs and lots of other critters said large bales of timothy hay are a lot cheaper, and hence we ended up with a lovely plastic bin inside our front door that held an entire bale of hay for our pigs, bringing our timothy hay costs down significantly. And making our front entryway quite lovely indeed.

At the time of their arrival, though, I was shocked at how much one could spend on a guinea pig. I was mentally listing other things I could do with the $600 a year that the upkeep of a pig would cost when I heard Elizabeth say, "All we have to do is put the pigs in their new home."

The thing about our two new charges is that they apparently hadn't been handled much, because when Elizabeth reached into the aquarium to grab the brown and white one—which she named Lincoln—he made this teeth-gnashing sound that, coming from a fuzzy animal weighing a mere pound or so, was nonetheless intimidating. Elizabeth gathered up another shot of courage, but going after the black and white one with pink ears—which she named Pinky—resulted in Pinky running off in an oinking snit. Mark solved this problem by lifting the lid on the new metal cage, putting the aquarium inside the new cage and gently tipping the aquarium on its side. In short order, the two pigs were scrambling about their new cage, squealing, pushing, shoving and literally running into the side of the cage and into the plastic hut.

We let the pigs alone for a bit, got online and learned that some guinea pigs like fresh fruit and vegetables, that they live an average of four to eight years, and—. And that's all I remember, because upon hearing that they live up to eight years, I realized that five years from the date of their arrival, Elizabeth would be going to college and the pigs were not likely to go with her. Indeed, I had just taken in two pigs whose survival and spoiling would fall to me.

Of course, I should have realized this right off, because Elizabeth lived with her mother and we only saw her every other weekend. She took good care of the pigs when she was around, but the thing is, guinea pigs need daily attention and care. And since I'd stepped up to the proverbial plate for the other animals Mark had always wanted, well, the pigs were just another interesting addition. They're pretty easy to take care of compared to, say, ferrets, especially since our guinea pigs were afraid of pretty much everything. Okay, everything.

I know this because after the first week, when it was time to scoop out the contents of their cage and replace it with fresh bedding, it was not easy. After removing the plastic hut and food container, I pondered two ways to remove the soiled bedding: one, remove the bedding with the pigs outside of the cage, or two, remove the bedding with the pigs running around inside the cage. To give the pigs a change of scenery, I decided to put them on the floor. It went something like this:

I reached in to get Lincoln, but he wiggled his surprisingly muscular body out of my grasp and ran away squealing.

More determined, I grabbed onto Pinky. He squealed like I was going to kill him, but this time I held on tighter and watched his chubby, little feet run in place as I lowered him to the floor. When I let go of him, he stood there frozen in place, his sides heaving in and out. I returned to the cage, made another grab at Lincoln, held on tighter than before, and lowered his squealing self to the floor. He, too, stood there unmoved.

In response to all the commotion, Dusty, the Angel Pup, came around the corner. I told him to sit, which he did after a moment's hesitation. I grabbed the blue dust pan I'd purchased on a whim a few weeks earlier, and using it as a scoop, began removing the old bedding. I scooped, checked on the pigs, scooped, and checked on Dusty. Everything went well except for the fact that the guinea pigs did not move a muscle during the five minutes I cleaned out their cage.

The bedding replaced, I boldly grabbed Lincoln and returned him to the cage, and then I grabbed Pinky and placed him inside. I cleaned their hut, removed the pulverized bits of food that rimmed their food dish, checked their water bottles and made sure both the top and side doors were shut. I was relieved when the pigs were both secured in their cage, though kind of sad that they were so afraid of new surroundings that they'd likely spend their entire lives in their cage.

While it didn't take me long to realize that the pigs were afraid of everything, it didn't take *them* long to train me to feed them every time I walked past their cage. Since their cage was by the front door, every time I let the dogs out or in, I had to walk by the pigs and in response, the pigs started "wheek"ing in stereo. To make this unpleasant sound go away as quickly as possible, I discovered I had to give them something they liked to eat, like a piece of celery, a strawberry, some lettuce, or a couple of tomato slices. They liked most vegetables and even though lettuce was said to give some guinea pigs diarrhea, ours inhaled the stuff without any kind of intestinal trouble. In no time, whenever I let the dogs out, I found myself walking to the refrigerator to see what fresh veggie I could offer the pigs. I also soon found myself shopping for them at the grocery store, making comments like, "Oh, I wonder if the pigs would like kale?"

One night within the first month of our pigs taking residence at our front entryway, I was waiting for the dogs to come back inside. I had given the pigs some tomato slices which they were ignoring. They were just standing around their cage and I was bored, so I opened the cage door to see if it might be possible to actually pet one of them. I stuck my hand out and as I brought my hand closer and closer to Pinky, he stood there, unmoving. I was thinking I might actually be able to pet the little bugger until, at the moment I made contact with the fur on his head, he jerked up and backwards at the same time and went squealing off to the plastic hut. Surprised by Pinky's reaction and a bit confused, when Lincoln approached me, I did the same thing. Lincoln stood there, unmoving, as my hand approached, and upon making contact, reacted the same way. I came to the conclusion that the old phrase "don't buy a pig in a poke" is indeed sound advice, because more than one poke of our pigs proved they were blind.

Tip #27: Every animal—including rodents— has its own personality.

Unbeknownst to me, Mark's ambition was to fill the void left by the fuzzy ferrets, and the guinea pigs were just the start. Shortly after the pigs joined us, Mark quit his job with the State of Michigan to warp the minds of biology students at Alma College, where, unfortunately for me, they feed gerbils, mice and hamsters to snakes. I know this because within months after Professor Mark started working at the college, he came home with this two-inch long, fuzzy, orange-tan, mouse-like thing that looked like it had stuck its foot in a light socket.

"It's a dwarf hamster," he explained. "Isn't he just the cutest?"

"After you, yes. And he came from?"

"The lab at the college."

"As in, a lab where they experiment with animals? Because, I don't want some weird virus in the house that causes women to grow third boobs or anything."

"No, these were bred to feed to snakes. But a third boob could be fun."

"'These'?" I asked, ignoring his anatomical comment. "As in, there's more?"

"Oh, yes. This was just the cutest."

I knew I was doomed. I knew if there were more cute, dwarf hamsters at the college, there would be more in my house. "But, um, if you bring one or two or three home, won't the college just keep producing more of these things anyway to feed to the snakes?"

"Maybe. But at least I can save a few."

I had no further argument, so asked, "And this one's name is?"

"Hammy."

"Hammy the Hamster. You *are* cute."

I'd never had a dwarf hamster before—or mice or gerbils—and I had no idea that most married biologists keep their mice, gerbils and hamsters in cages and aquariums on their kitchen counter. Why on the counter?

"Because if they're in our bedroom, they'll stink it up. If they're in the dining room, we might eat them. If they're in the basement, we'll forget about them. Besides," Mark concluded, "we'll want to see them every day because they're so cute."

At the time he spoke in plural, only Hammy existed, but within a week Hammy was joined by a white mouse that Conrad named Aldacar. Mark gave this mouse to Conrad and within two months it died, making me once again fearful of growing a third breast. Aldacar was soon followed by three other mice that Mark kept in separate cages on the counter. This brought the fuzzy-critters-on-the-counter count to four.

Soon, an old aquarium appeared containing two black and white fuzzies that looked like mice on steroids.

"What are those?"

"Gerbils."

"They look like what a kangaroo mouse would look like. I mean, look at those bent back legs. I bet they could leap a foot into the air."

"I'm glad you like them."

"Oh, I'm in love with all of them. And I love my new kitchen. The colors all go together so well. And they bring out the overall duct tape motif of the house."

Our kitchen isn't large to begin with, and with the animal cages and aquariums on the counter, we had approximately three square feet of counter space to prepare food on. Since the housing inspector had assigned me the roof-gutter-tree-trimming duties, Mark was the man of the kitchen, so the fact that the kitchen had little counter space was really his problem. And if he didn't mind, why should I?

So I didn't mind, really, until my mother stopped over, and, upon seeing the cages on the counter raised her eyebrows, laughed out loud and said, "I'm sure glad you don't live with me, because there's no way you'd have animals on the counter in my house."

I told her I was glad I didn't live with her, too.

Later, my sister called, and when I told her about my new family members and where we kept them, she said she was glad she didn't live with us and would likely decline any invitations to dinner. I told her I was glad she didn't live here, too, and that she wasn't invited to dinner anyway. Ever.

On the other end of the spectrum was my brother, Lloyd, who thought it was simply an inconvenience not having any counter space because it was occupied by gerbils, even though he didn't know what a gerbil really is.

Years later, he showed up at our house with his two young daughters, who thought it was cool that we had little fuzzy critters on our kitchen counter.

On the far, far end of the spectrum was my dad's wife, Norma, who couldn't keep herself from fondling each one of the fuzzies in turn. I seriously thought she was going to rub the fur off Hammy's back and had to ask her to put him away before he went bald.

The gerbils were kind of cute, though not as cute as Hammy, and their behavior was rather interesting. While mice sometimes squeak when they get a particularly yummy treat—pumpkin seeds being a favorite—the gerbils *always* squeak when they get food and also when fighting over it. Gerbils also thump on the floor of their cages to communicate with each other. I don't know what the thumping means, exactly, but I'm guessing it's anything from, "Hi, Jerkweed, I'm still here, are you?" to, "Hey, I think we can sucker that lady into feeding us again."

Indeed it was fun having critters on my kitchen counter because there was always a fuzzy cute thing to greet me every time I went into the kitchen. Conrad really must have liked it, because he soon named our home Rancho Rodento. He also wrote a song that went:

Rancho Rodento, it's made for you and me,
Rancho Rodento, we're happy as can be! Hey!

**Tip #28: It is important (although not easy)
to know a boy gerbil from a girl gerbil.**

In addition to not having counter space or an understanding of the language of gerbils, the other problem with gerbils is the size of their genitals. I mean, the size of their genitals is right for them, but they're so small it's hard for humans to differentiate one sex from the other. At least that's Mark's excuse for putting the two gerbils together. And, well, let's just say that the two gerbils became five quite unexpectedly. That led to having to separate the boys from the girls, which, after visiting a pet store, we figured out is done by grabbing the animal by its tail, looking at its private parts and making sure that the gerbils with two holes close together are kept separated from the gerbils whose two orifices are further apart. We also had to separate the dad and son gerbil from each other because the two boys nipped and chased each other and it wasn't a pretty thing to watch at all. Soon there were seven cages on my kitchen counter.

Now, gerbils apparently come equipped with teeth that need constant filing and they chew anything they can find, including their cages. If you're not paying attention, you may one day discover gerbils running around your house. Or in my case, hiding from the dog behind the refrigerator.

I knew something was up when I came home from work to find Dusty by the refrigerator, wagging his tail and pumping his front legs up and down. Since he'd never begged by the refrigerator before, I was immediately suspicious. I peered down at the two-inch crack between the kitchen counter and the fridge, and saw a really impressive dust bunny, a couple of expired coupons and a dinosaur refrigerator magnet from Wall Drug, South Dakota. I looked back at the still begging Dusty, then leaned over the back of the counter to look behind the fridge. My eyes met the surprised look of the black and white gerbil we had named Mama Gerbil sitting on the refrigerator coils. At least, I inferred that it was a surprised look. See, gerbils and mice don't typically possess the ability to change their expression, although we did have one mouse that scrunched his eyes and mouth up at food he didn't like. So, really, Mama Gerbil couldn't open her eyes real big to show me if she was surprised, any more than she could let me know if she was afraid, hungry, tired, or having the time of her life hanging around the refrigerator coils. She could only flinch when the refrigerator suddenly kicked into gear and began humming.

As I pondered what to do, I had some weird thoughts: *If she fries herself on the back of the fridge, we won't have to worry about her anymore; if she comes out at night and Dusty pounces on her, we don't have to worry about her anymore; if she sneaks off and disappears somewhere else in the house, we won't have to worry about her any more. Hm. That's some pattern, isn't it?*

Then I got logical—a trait I was proud to maintain even after 18 years in state government—and realized that a gerbil's brain is slightly larger than microscopic. Mama Gerbil's goal had been to chew her teeth down and she'd inadvertently chewed through her cage because Mark and I hadn't paid much attention to her teeth. She ended up behind the refrigerator because any other way off the counter meant instant death.

I figured the first thing to do was tie the local predators, Dusty and Little Dipper, outside. Then I checked the cage to see if the other two female gerbils had also escaped. The tan one—who remained nameless—was still chewing on the cage from the inside. The other one—a nearly perfect clone of Mama Gerbil and also nameless—was on the counter climbing up one of the male gerbil's cages. I grabbed the Mama Gerbil look-alike by her tail, placed her in her cage, and duct taped the tiny hole that Mama Gerbil had made. I was about to turn my attention to Mama Gerbil when I suddenly remembered a really sick story told by a college roommate who had placed a sticky strip on a small board to catch a mouse in her house; how she couldn't peel the mouse's feet off the sticky strip, so placed the board into the Rouge River upside down, cruelly drowning the mouse. With this image fresh in my mind, I stuck a second piece of duct tape inside the cage facing the other piece of tape so the gerbils didn't get stuck to the tape.

With two of the females caged again temporarily, I was on the verge of a brilliant solution to getting Mama Gerbil out from the refrigerator when Mark came home from work. "Why are the dogs outside in the rain?" was his first question, followed by, "What are you doing with your head behind the refrigerator?"

I explained the dilemma and what I had done so far, and that I was about to block the right side of the fridge so that if and when Mama Gerbil came down from her hiding spot she would run down the left side of the fridge.

"And then what?"

"Then you grab her."

His eyes nearly convulsed as they rolled to the back of his head and he said, "Yeah, right, like that'll work." Yet amazingly, that's pretty much what happened. I blocked off the right side, Mark grabbed a Wheat Thin from the cupboard and held it to the back of the fridge, and Mama Gerbil crawled down from the back of the fridge and walked out along the two-inch crack. She was almost within reach when she suddenly flinched and ran back to the fridge.

So, we tried again, and this time, we placed a cookie sheet on either side of the two-inch crack. Mama Gerbil came out from behind the fridge a few minutes later, and to keep her from running back to the fridge again, as soon as she cleared the back of the two cookie sheets, I, lying on the counter like most people chasing gerbils, slowly squeezed the far ends of the two cookies sheets together. Mama Gerbil's only option was to keep going towards Mark, who grabbed her and picked her up.

"See?" I said. "Just like I planned it."

We tucked her away, and after eating chicken chow mein (which caused us to ponder whether gerbils taste like chicken), we went off to a new pet store where we found a bargain of a cage for our lady gerbil friends. While the new cage had plastic tubes and an enclosed plastic area at the top, likely meant for gerbils to nest in, the bottom was a solid piece of plastic and the sides were metal. With less chewable plastic and fewer opportunities for escape, Mark was confident that this new cage would hold his female gerbils.

Tip #29: Rodents will chew whatever is handy to gnaw on.

Within 48 hours, the ladies had chewed ragged teeth marks in the plastic container at the top of the new cage. It was the same container they liked to poop in, and I found it quite disgusting that they went up there to defecate and think, "Gee, while we're here, let's chew on the plastic!" But that's what they did.

I sat down with a cold beer and pondered what I would like to chew if I were a gerbil. Plastic did not make it to the top of my list. Apple wood came to mind, but that's only because a friend had raised rabbits and they liked apple wood. But how many pieces of apple wood could I hack off my apple tree before it would die? And for gerbils, no less.

I was batting around other ideas when I saw an empty cereal box by the microwave that a certain Somebody had failed to put in with the other recyclable materials. I pulled at the ends, ripped off a chunk of it, shoved it into the cage door and prodded the ladies down the tube. Within 30 seconds, all three of the gerbils were happily chewing the box; within ten minutes, the box had been chewed into shredded bits equal to that made by the best paper shredder.

From then on, part of our daily routine included finding cereal boxes, cracker boxes, Kleenex boxes and other boxes of similar consistency, ripping them into large chunks and sticking pieces into the gerbil cages. When we ran out of cereal boxes or snack boxes, we gave the gerbils our junk mail. No matter the time of the day or night, chewing commenced almost immediately upon receiving the munchable material. With up to five gerbils chewing at the same time, it sounded not unlike several telegraph machines.

In addition to not realizing that more people should have gerbils instead of paper shredders, I also had no idea that gerbils, mice and dwarf hamsters all have their own personalities, and their own likes and dislikes. The two white mice exercised on their exercise wheels, but while one of them pooped somewhere other than on their wheel, the other one pooped and exercised at the same time. Some of the mice and gerbils came up to the side of the cage to get food from us, a typical favorite being Wheat Thins, while others ran around their cage to find the treat we put in for them.

I also discovered that mice can learn from each other. Our two white males had discovered the advantage of coming to the side of the cage to get a treat from us. Then Mark rescued another mouse that he kept up at Alma College for several months where the mouse did not come up to the side of the cage to get treats. One day, for reasons unknown to me, Mark figured his Alma mouse would be better off at home with us. Within a week, the new mouse had learned from the other two mice that good things come to those who go to the side of their cage, and he, too, greeted us as soon as he heard the crinkle of the inside of the Wheat Thin box.

While these creatures were fascinating in weird ways, when the kitchen counter was covered with eight small cages containing small rodents I said, "Enough, please. We have enough to take care of."

But I knew it was just a matter of time.

Tip #30: Some pets show up when and where you least expect them.

CHAPTER 6

Fuzzies He Didn't Know
He'd Always Wanted

In early September 2005, right after we settled Conrad at Michigan State University to start his freshman year, I went out the basement door to find an old birdbath that I knew was under our deck somewhere. The underside of our deck houses an amazing array of kayaks and cages, old plant pots, an old go-kart, pieces of a three-tube bird feeder Mark won't throw away, and sawhorses that have never sawn anything. I was poking around the junk when there appeared from near the kayaks this gray and white fuzzy thing that made a mew-like noise. I held perfectly still, and as it slowly approached, I determined it to be a skinny bobcat-like kitten. After several minutes, I took a step towards the mewing little fur ball and it ran off under the pile of cages and kayaks.

Well, that isn't a good place for a skinny kitty, said I to myself. So I ran to the store for a small squishy bag of Tender Vittles, two cans of two different brands of cat food, a small bag of cat treats, and, in case none of that worked, some cream. With $15 worth of kitten attractant, I took a plate outside, dumped food from each package I'd purchased, and ended up with a mound of food as big as the kitten itself. As soon as I was done yanking open cans, tapping a fork to get the food out, and ripping open soft packages of gooey food, the kitten emerged from behind a kayak.

I slowly sat down on the ground near the food and was mid-squat when the kitten scurried back behind the kayak. Thinking perhaps it only understood cat, I started meowing at the little thing. In seconds, the kitten appeared and began approaching carefully, one step at a time, looking at me the entire time. As he approached, I asked where it had come from, how old it was, where its mother was, and what kind of mother would have dumped him out here all by himself? The little fuzzy didn't have anything to say in return, but my jibber-jabber apparently made him feel confident enough to sit down in front of the plate and eat. As he ate in wolfing bites, I contemplated grabbing him, contemplated whether I'd get bitten if I did grab him, contemplated whether getting bitten would make me froth at the mouth and want to chew on Mark, contemplated the likelihood of Mark saying I could bring him inside. Undecided on all accounts and after running out of questions for the little kitten, I stood up slowly and the kitten scampered off behind the kayak again.

I left the kitten to eat what it would the first day, hoping it would survive the night under our deck. The next day, I flung the unconsolidated leftover food-mush into the yard for the local crows, left a more reasonable portion of new food for the tiny waif and sat down. Within seconds, the mewing creature emerged from behind the cages and kayaks. As before, I jabbered on mindlessly as it ate. While its tiny bobcat-like face was buried in the food, I reached out very slowly to pet the kitten. My hand was still a foot away when the kitten bolted part way back to the cages. But it didn't disappear. Perhaps still hungry, it turned around, waited for me to do something else, and when it was clear I would keep my hands to myself, it slowly, cautiously returned for more food. I sat long enough to see the kitten fill its little tummy, and stood to let my new friend try to eek out one more night on its own.

The next evening, as the kitten ate, I reached out very slowly, arm outstretched, blood rushing to the flabby part of my arm and weighing it down, my eyes going from the kitten's eyes to its claws, whispering, "Please don't bite me." Since the kitten gave no signs to indicate "danger!" I finally touched the kitten's head. And this time, instead of running away, it purred. The purring didn't last long, and, as if surprised by its own reaction, the kitten turned toward the cages and disappeared.

That evening, Mark asked if I was going to keep feeding the kitty, or if I was going to catch it. I told him I was going to catch it. He bet me I couldn't. We settled on a six-pack of beer.

The next evening, temperatures were forecasted to drop to freezing. With Mark happily nested on the couch and pondering what kind of beer I would buy him, I brought a small animal carrier outside with me, opened the door, and put cat food inside. I squatted down and waited only a few seconds before the kitten came over. When it cautiously put its face inside the cage, I shoved it gently from behind and shut the door.

The kitten mewed as I carried it inside and placed it on Mark's lap. "No way!" was the first answer, followed by, "You are so lucky."

"And thirsty, too. I'd like Heineken, please."

Mark followed me and our two curious dogs toward the bedrooms. We went into Elizabeth's room, shut the dogs out, and put the cage on the floor. When we opened the door to the cage, the kitten skirted away between Elizabeth's bed and the wall.

I dove on top of the bed and urged the little thing towards Mark, who, meanwhile, was reaching toward it with his giant hand and saying, "It's dead if it bites me."

And then it happened: Mark had the tiny kitten in his hand and all we heard was the sound of a motorized purr machine rattling and humming away.

Mark said, "What a cutie," and his eyes were lit as he petted the kitten and looked it over. Up close, the kitten looked like a tiny bobcat with a white ruff under its chin and white feet. "It's really skinny. Good thing we got him when we did."

"We?" I looked at him.

I left Mark to bond with the kitten and went in search of my very first litter box and bag of litter, which, amazingly enough, a kitten uses right away. None of that puppy-like "Let's go outside and go potty!" stuff and wiping up pee. I wondered why I'd never had a kitten before. Oh, yes. My mother disliked cats.

Getting a simple bag of kitty litter wasn't simple because of the options: Clay, crystals, or natural and biodegradable? If clay, then clumping or non-clumping? Scented or unscented? Small bag or big bag? To my credit, I only took 20 minutes to decide on a 40-pound bag of Tidy Cats non-clumping kitty litter, which was the cheapest.

With my first bag of kitty litter in hand, I returned home to find Mark reclined on the couch with the kitten lying on top of him.

"You should probably call the vet," Mark greeted me. "You know, in case he has worms or something."

I've had unprovoked nightmares about worms before, so set up an appointment the next day at the Haslett Animal Hospital. Getting the kitten—whom I named Purrkins—into the animal carrier was a breeze and he was as quiet as a mouse at the veterinarian hospital and sat patiently inside the cage, waiting his turn. Behind the counter where the clerks were happily writing up bills, was a cage containing three other kittens that looked like Purrkins but without the white feet. The assistant behind the counter explained that, "Someone found those kittens by a dumpster and, rather than turn them into the Humane Society where animals sometimes get put to sleep, they brought them here. Over time, we hope to find them good homes."

Purrkins was an instant celebrity because he had fleas, ticks and a rare case of feline lice. In fact, Purrkins was the first case of kitty lice this vet had seen, and she was so fascinated by this discovery, she showed the lice under a microscope to all three of her technicians, as well as to Mark, who gets a bizarre kick out of seeing tiny parasites wiggle. Mark was also a hit, because between glances at wiggly lice, he presented convincing arguments to the vet's assistants that Purrkins was a Norwegian Forest Cat rather than the common tabby. I, meanwhile, was waiting in the lobby humming to myself so as not to think about fleas, ticks, lice and shots.

A few shots and a hundred dollars later, our kitten was on his way home again. And within a few days we had a healthy happy kitten that terrorized our two dogs by leaping out at them from behind chairs as they walked by, and batting at their faces while they slept. Purrkins also had an affinity for the flushing toilet, and ran hell-bent across the house and into the bathroom whenever he heard it flush. He'd come to a stop on the blue throw rug at the base of the toilet and, with his back feet planted on the rug, place his front feet on the lip of the bowl and watch the water go round and round in the bowl. Fearful that I would awake one morning and find a drowned kitten in the toilet, I suggested to Mark that he put the seat AND lid down.

"I'll do my best," he promised.

His best was two days.

Within a few months, Purrkins was coordinated enough to sprint across the house, leap into the air and come to a stop on top of the toilet seat. He'd stick his whole head inside the toilet to get a close-up look at the swirling water. Months later, after he'd trained me to hold a cup of fresh water for him to sip out of while he sat on the bathroom counter, Purrkins would still look up from the cup of water to watch the swirling toilet water.

When he was about six months old, Purrkins leapt onto my computer desk and—because I'd left my laptop open a crack—stuck his little clawed feet into the computer and flicked off the space bar, K key and the A key. I found all three keys under our 8x12 foot rug in the living room, and was able to replace the A key by snapping it back into place. The K key was cracked, but after a little epoxy to keep the cracked key from splitting permanently into two pieces, I snapped it back into place as well. The space key, though in one piece, was apparently missing the spring that went with it, because it never did work correctly again. I called Dell and asked for a new space bar. They said I had to buy a new keyboard, which would cost over $100. Instead, I attached a separate keyboard to the back of my laptop, making it more like a desktop, thanks to my kitten.

Because of the keyboard mishap and the fact that needle-like claws are a danger to our dogs, mice, and valuables, we had Purrkins' front paws de-clawed. In case Mark had ideas about raising kittens, I also added neutering to the surgical order. These were the only conditions for sharing our home with a kitten whose natural instincts were to hunt and kill. Oh, and being rid of his fleas, ticks and lice. Call me a bad biologist, but I've never cared for fleas, ticks or lice, even the ones wiggling under a microscope.

Little did I know that something even more gross and wiggly was about to come into my life.

Tip #31: Fleas jump more than rabbits.

In October, less than a month later, I took a week off from work to get caught up on my writing and bond with Purrkins. Mid-week, I went on a bike ride at the Rose Lake Wildlife area with Roger, a friend I envy because unlike me, he's a retired state employee, not a working one. The hour-long ride wasn't particularly memorable, until I got off my mountain bike at the parking lot and saw a white something out of the corner of my eye. It was a rabbit, and its eyes were jet black and surrounded with Marilyn Manson-inspired eyeliner. To its left, about fifteen feet away, was a gray and white rabbit.

"Do you see what I see?" I asked Roger.

"Rabbits," he said. "Cute rabbits."

In all my years outside I hadn't seen wild rabbits that looked like these because they were *domestic* rabbits. I stalked the white one like a decrepit cat and it ran off. Not to be outsmarted by one rabbit, I strolled up to the gray and white one, and, upon getting a few feet away, noticed that it had a messed up nose, as if it had been in a fight and its nose was still healing over. I reached out, grabbed at the gray and white bunny and was surprised when, a second later, I held the bunny in my hand. As I held it close to my chest so it wouldn't struggle to get away, Roger opened the door of my car where I happened to have a box. We put the bunny in the box, folded the corners of the lid, and shut the door.

"What are you going to do with him?"

"I haven't a clue. But he won't survive out here come winter, so—."

Out of the corner of my eye, I saw something black moving on the berm. It was a black rabbit with white trim. "I'm bettin' I'll be back to try to catch more."

On the way home it occurred to me that I knew nothing about rabbits except that they hopped and liked carrots. Or was it just Bugs Bunny that liked carrots?

At home, I left the bunny in the box in my car while I tried to herniate myself by going under our deck and moving a giant rectangular cage out of the way to uncover the large ferret cage and, finally, the small cage with screen mesh for sides—you know, the one that Mark thought Coco couldn't get out of? After I brought out the cage, I went to retrieve the rabbit. I pulled back the folded corners of the box, ready to pounce on the bunny if it jumped, but was surprised when it allowed me to pick it up and place it inside the cage without a struggle. I watched for a moment, half expecting it to go ballistic inside the cage. It had, after all, lived freely "in the wild" for who knows how long.

When the bunny calmly walk-hopped around inside the cage, I set about finding a dish for water. With a half dozen dishes scattered about the garage, I selected a small ceramic one and went about pulling a few dandelions. Minutes later, Mark returned from work and, without saying hello, asked what in the world a bunny was doing in the cage. When I told him there were others running around Rose Lake, he said we had to get them because they weren't likely to survive.

We returned to Rose Lake with fish landing nets, old

clothes and empty stomachs. In the parking lot were several other cars. Two belonged to my co-workers, Brenda and Megan, who had also somehow heard about the rabbits. Another belonged to a woman nobody knew, who said somebody had dumped off fifteen rabbits three days prior; five had already been rounded up. With nets in hand, we had rabbits to get, so nobody bothered asking the woman's name, what colors and kinds of rabbits had already been caught, or what had happened to them.

We spent the next hour or so running around like idiots, chasing bunnies with landing nets that kept getting snagged on rose thorn and other nasty vegetation. Each time we had our nets poised to nab a rabbit, the varmint hopped out of reach as its pursuer quietly cursed and untangled their net or clothes. The unknown woman caught one and drove away with it, never to be seen again by us. We didn't catch any more that first evening.

Over the course of the next few weeks the rest of us returned several more times to round up more rabbits. I told my mother about the bunny roundup and she joined us one evening in a new pair of jeans, a sweater and shining white tennis shoes—the flat ones cheerleaders wore when I was younger and trying to grow up. When I accused my mother of showing up just to watch me run around like an idiot, she assured me she would help out. And she did. By standing on the berm, looking down at me and my friends and saying, "Oh, there goes the black and white one!" or, "Oh, you could have had that brown one if your net hadn't gotten tangled."

Overall, we rounded up five more of the rabbits, two of which Brenda took home. Mark and I took three, including a small all-black bunny, a small black one with silver trim, and the gray and white one with the crusty nose.

"Could whatever he has be contagious?" I asked Mark, referring the gray and white rabbit.

"If I knew what it had, I could answer that question."

"So, you don't know."

"I wouldn't say that."

"Well, we need to find someone who does know. I mean, really knows."

"Of course."

Since the staff at Soldan's hadn't let us down yet, I thought perhaps they would be able to help us with the rabbits. By this point, Mark and I were regular customers, buying dog food and cat food, bedding for all sorts of animals, and corn and sunflower seed for squirrels, mallard ducks and songbirds. When I asked for a bunny expert, I was led to Betsy, a 20-something-year-old worker who had raised lots of rabbits. Betsy assured us rabbits were easy to take care of. She shared hints and tidbits of advice as she led us around the store for a bale of timothy hay, rabbit pellet food, rabbit Mardi Gras in a help-yourself bin, and chew sticks.

"Do you know what kind of rabbits they are?"

"The gray and white variety, the all-black variety and the black with silver trim variety," I said.

"I can't wait to see them," Betsy said, trying not to laugh.

I described the gray and white one's funky nose and Betsy suggested it might be sick and should be separated from the others "just in case." As I told her that we'd put antibiotic on the bunny's nose, she led us to cages. We soon had a black folding cage to add to our other rabbit goods.

"Do you know what gender they are?" she asked.

Mark looked at me. I looked at Mark. He said, "They won't tell us."

Betsy laughed. "If you bring them in, I'll help you figure

that out. And you should do that pretty soon, unless you want more rabbits."

Before Mark could respond, I said, "We do not want more rabbits. We'll bring them in. Thank you."

As Mark went on about why we might want to think about raising rabbits, that the rabbits might have already mated, that if we were lucky one of them was already pregnant, I wandered to the counter shaking my head praying, "Heaven help me."

On the way home, we stopped at Target to purchase several unbranded boxes of oat and grain cereal. Megan later topped off the bunny diet by bringing to work several apple tree branches and a bucket of fresh apples.

We kept our three rabbits in separate cages in the garage for the first few days: the gray and white one in the Velcro-sided cage; the all-black one in a small, old ferret cage; and the black one with the white trim in the new cage. For most people who don't use their garages for cars anyway, keeping rabbits in a garage would have been good enough. But since I'm not most people—and because Mark said the rabbits wouldn't survive outside—I decided that a garage was enough like outside to be bad for the rabbits, so I moved the rabbits into a spare bedroom.

Surely, not one of my better ideas.

Two days later, as I was putting fresh dandelions into their cages, I saw a tick the size of a small tarantula striding across the bedroom floor. Almost at the same moment, Brenda called to tell me that she and a buddy of ours had spent an hour taking ticks off Brenda's rabbits with tweezers. She said the rabbits also had fleas.

I'm all about sharing my house with other creatures as long as their primary mode of living isn't crawling and sucking or chewing on other animals. Upon discovering that "we" had crawlies, I had those rabbit cages back in the garage in record time, even if there are no records for such an event. Itching all the way, I ran back to Betsy the Bunny Expert and asked her what might kill the crawlies on my rabbits. She recommended something called Reptile Relief by a company named Natural Chemistry, and said she'd used it on day-old rabbits with no ill effect.

"But rabbits are not reptiles," I whispered.

"But it works and doesn't hurt rabbits," she whispered back. "Just ignore the name," and shooed me out the door.

What a fun evening! Betsy had advised that the rabbits would be particularly shivery when the Reptile Relief went to work, so we rounded up three shoeboxes from our disaster of a house, cut holes in them and stuck one in each of the cages on top of a wad of hay. That done, we took each rabbit out of its cage and I sprayed it while Mark held the rabbit. We both rubbed the rabbit's fur to spread the Reptile Relief around. Before putting each rabbit back in its cage, we made sure it had plenty of hay, food and water, and made sure the shoeboxes were big enough for them to hide inside.

With our new charges all sprayed and fighting off their tiny enemies, I returned to the bedroom and sprayed Reptile Relief on every inch of carpet and everything else in the bedroom. An hour later, I vacuumed the bedroom and, suspecting that some of the fleas and ticks might just hunker down when the floor was vibrating from the vacuum cleaner, I vacuumed an adjacent room before returning to The Bunny Room for another vacuum. Good thing I did, because a behemoth tick the size of a small crab was wandering across the floor. After sucking it up, I emptied the vacuum cleaner bag into a garbage bag, sprayed the inside of both bags with Reptile Relief, tied the garbage bag closed and left it outside by the garage door. In the event the tick survived being sprayed twice, vacuumed and suffocated in plastic, odds were, it'd find its way to some warm-blooded creature outside, rather than inside my house.

That night, I closed my eyes and could see giant crawling ticks. I rolled over and saw giant fleas. I rolled over again and Mark asked, "What the heck is the problem?" When I told him, his response was to run his fingers down my leg.

The next day, Brenda called with a sad story about already having two bunnies from a previous rescue effort near her house a year or so ago, and how her two bunnies were set in their ways and not getting along with the two new ones. She asked if I would take her two bunnies. She had temporarily taken in the small brown one that looked the most like a wild rabbit, and the white one with the black eyeliner that I had first seen while riding my bike. We were out of cages by this point, so Brenda's two rabbits went in the old multi-level ferret cage together. After spraying Brenda's two bunnies with Reptile Relief, Mark and I returned to Soldan's for one more cage, separated Brenda's bunnies and went to bed, thinking once again about fleas and ticks.

That night, I closed my eyes and saw tiny, white kitty lice looking at me with their pin-sized eyes from the split-ends of my hair. One recognized me and said, "Mom!" Soon all the tiny kitty lice were calling to me. I saw bloated ticks the size of silver dollars walking across my bed, and I could hear them making this sick slurping sound. Tiny fleas kicked with glee as they hopped from my head to my hand and down to my crotch. I was convinced my bed was infested, and no logic could persuade me otherwise. I itched all over, yet didn't want to scratch certain places that did itch. Quietly, trying not to wake Mark, who seemed unaware of the perils, I got up and showered vigorously to make the crawly feeling go away.

When I had finally settled back into bed and was about to drift off to sleep, Mark said, "You missed one," and ran his fingers down my leg. This time, I waited until I heard the little snort-snore that indicated he was about to fall asleep. When I ran my fingers down Mark's legs, he sat straight up in bed, then wiggled and shook and scratched himself all in one spastic motion. "Touché."

Tip #32: An experienced pet owner is worth their weight in gold.

Thanks to Betsy the Bunny Expert, within 48 hours of infesting our house and brain cells, all the crawlies were gone and we had five flea-free, tick-free fuzzies. The bedroom was free of crawlies as well, and they never migrated to Dusty, Dipper, Purrkins, the guinea pigs, or the numerous mice on our kitchen counter. They also did not make it into our bedroom.

When the rabbits were all cured of their crawling critters, we put them all in two boxes and drove them back to Betsy the Bunny Expert, who identified their genders by tipping them on their backs and fondling this nubby space between their legs. After identifying the genders of the first two rabbits, Betsy asked if Mark wanted to take a turn identifying the gender of the next one and he politely declined with, "Thanks, but we like having *you* fondle them."

Thanks to Betsy the Bunny Fondling Expert, we learned the brown bunny, gray and white bunny, and black with silver trim bunny were all females; the white one and all-black one were both males. We put them in two boxes, separated by gender.

"Don't leave the males together very long," Betsy said. "Because males often fight."

We nodded and said we were only ten minutes from home, that the rabbits hadn't shown a single sign of aggression, and should be okay. The boxes didn't thump or wiggle as we carried them to the car, and all was quiet in the back seat until we pulled into the driveway. Suddenly, a scrambling, scratching sound became a THUMP!, and a sound like a muffled scream. Mark and I bolted from the car, opened up the back door, pulled back the corners of the box the males were in and while Mark grabbed the black one, I grabbed the white one. The box contained a little blood and a bit of fur from both rabbits. The back legs of the white bunny were splotched with orangey-red blood. The black one had a patch of fur missing on its back, but not down to the skin.

"Boy, that was stupid of us," Mark sighed.

I followed him into the garage. He tucked the black one into a cage and said, "Let me put the females away and then we'll check out the white one a little closer."

He returned to the car, grabbed the box with the females, and tucked them each away.

"Maybe get a wet rag so we can wipe the blood off him," I suggested.

Mark went inside, met the barking dogs with a "Be quiet!" and returned with a wet rag. He helped me turn the white bunny onto his back, wiped its legs off and inspected a small wound near its genitals. After applying a dab of antibiotic, we apologized to the white bunny and put him in his cage.

I glanced at each cage to make sure the doors were all shut, and to make sure they all had food and water. When I glanced at the black bunny, I said, "Mark, he looks like he has a lump on his neck."

"It may just be from where the white one bit him," Mark said.

I stepped closer, opened the cage and pulled back the fur to take a closer look. In addition to the bump, I saw a hole. Suddenly feeling sickly, I called Mark over, "Uh, honey? Can bunnies get botflies?"

"Any animal can get a botfly," he said. "Why, my sweetie pie?"

I pulled the fur back on the bunny's neck and said, "Please tell me—."

"Sweet!" Mark grinned. "That's really cool. You can see the hole in the rabbit's skin where its little butt spiracles stick out to breathe while its head—which is pointing inside the rabbit—is—."

"I don't need to know this," I stopped him. "What are we going to do?"

I knew of two options, the first of which is to let it hatch out and fly around and lay eggs, which turn into botfly larvae and wiggle around in some other animal. The other option—one I read in a chapter of *Tropical Nature* by Adrian Forsyth and Ken Miyata called "Jerry's Maggot" after a guy who let a botfly wiggle around under his skin until it hatched—was to put a very fresh piece of raw meat on the bunny and hope the botfly hopped onto the very fresh piece of meat.

"I'll get some tweezers," Mark said bouncing away like a rabbit. "You bring the bunny to the dining room where I can see better. We'll get that bugger out."

"Do what?" I couldn't imagine much that was more horrifying. "At the dining room table?"

To make it more horrific, Mark brought a vial with alcohol to the table.

"You're not going to save this botfly," I stated.

"Sure I am. This is really cool. This is real biology."

"This is disgusting."

Amazingly, the little bunny did not wiggle or try to get away. And he didn't seem to be particularly perturbed about having a live wiggling maggot in its neck. The rabbit wasn't wiggling on its back or trying to scratch its back. I mentioned this to Mark.

"Don't you think he'll be more comfortable with the botfly maggot out of its neck?"

"Yes. Okay, let's do this already."

I held the bunny firmly on the table and looked away. Mark was jabbering happily about how cool this was and that we should be videotaping this to show his bio students. He went on about the importance of getting the whole larvae out because leaving part of it inside the rabbit would mean we'd have to take him to a vet to get the head out, and in the meantime, the lower half of the maggot would be wiggling around until it died.

"I don't need to know this," I said again.

"Oh, you should see this. You can see the head of the maggot in the opening in the bunny."

"I'm thrilled for you." And of course, I *had* to look. Sure enough, the air hole the maggot had created for itself was large enough in the bunny's black fur so I could see something inside, something with "eyes" that were actually spiracles on its butt.

I felt woozy and started singing: "I'm a little happy grub, lookin' for a little love." The bunny wiggled ever so slightly and I looked at it to check on my grip just as Mark was pulling the maggot out of the bunny's neck. The maggot was pale white with ridges that had tiny hooks. At about ¼-inch thick, it seemed impossibly large for the small hole in the bunny's neck, and it was almost an inch long, which just isn't right for a small bunny. Worst of all—Mark had it in his hand and was talking to it.

"Hey, little fella. Hope you had fun inside the bunny."

As he talked, the maggot went back and forth from a straight line to a C-shape, as if doing sit-ups.

"I'm sorry," Mark continued as the maggot did its exercises, "but you're really cool and I've gotta share you with my students. So, it's pickling time for you." He dropped the maggot into the vial. The maggot wiggled in the alcohol, turned into a C one more time and stopped moving. I thought I would barf.

But the bunny was still in my hand and I swallowed down any thoughts of exposing my lunch to the light of day as Mark applied a dab of antibiotic to the small hole in the bunny's neck. He pushed the fur back into place, sat back and smiled. "That was amazing. I'm so glad I got the whole thing out."

"Me, too." I stood wearily, carried the still unaffected, unmoving bunny back to his cage in the garage, and tucked him safely away. When I returned to the dining room, Mark, still beaming from ear to ear, asked, "Did you find any more botfly larvae?"

"Yes, and I already got it out. And I ate it."

Mark laughed, "You'll never be able to out-gross me. I ate the one from the vial."

Tip #33: Some pets like being petted; some do not.

Because owning five rabbits wasn't exactly what we'd had in mind, I hung flyers at the Haslett Animal Hospital and Soldan's, with nice photos and great descriptions like, "Makes a Great Pet!" a statement that could be true, depending on the particular rabbit. I also talked them up at work as THE animal that people should own. Unfortunately, my coworkers are all suspicious in nature—or perhaps just suspicious of me—and the smartest amongst them asked why, if rabbits are THE animal of choice, I was giving them away.

Among the skeptics, though, was one coworker who knew of a bunny rescue person, which is a person who rescues bunnies AND knows how to take care of them. A woman named Deanna offered to take two of my bunnies, so I gave her the two females—the gray and white one with the funky nose and the tiny brown one. Deanna was a godsend, because it turned out the gray and white one's nose problem was not due to an injury, but because it had pneumonia and bronchitis. Deanna footed the bill for the four rounds of antibiotics it took to get the gray and white bunny back on the road to recovery. It soon became a very affectionate bunny and was later adopted by a mother and daughter looking for a snuggly pal.

The brown bunny—the one that looked like a small wild rabbit—turned into a little hormonal hellion. Last I knew, Deanna was going to get the brown bunny spayed in the hopes that doing so would turn the little she-devil into a nice little bunny again.

Meanwhile, Elizabeth had a friend that raised rabbits and had always wanted a black one, so we gave her the mostly black bunny and his black and white trimmed pal.

That left us with the white bunny, called a hot-tot (which is pronounced "ho-toe"). I named him Magic because he only allowed someone to touch him if they could perform some magic few people have figured out. And believe me, I tried. I sat on the floor perfectly still with my hand out. Magic came up to me, sniffed my hand and, when

I raised it to pet him, he turned and thumped at the same time before hopping away. I thought maybe I could touch him if I offered him something he liked, which included raisins, Multi-Grain Cheerios and his favorite—by the way he snatched it—a vanilla wafer. So, I sat and waited with the treat, Magic approached, took the treat and as I moved my hand from near his mouth to the top of his head he turned, thumped and bounced away. I soon tired of sitting around plotting ways to pet Magic, and figured that with two dogs, a cat and a husband, I had plenty of furry things that liked being petted.

While Magic hated being held or petted by me, Purrkins could "pet" Magic all he wanted. Purrkins' ploy was to sprawl himself out on the floor and wait for Magic to touch him, then bat at him gently with his front paws. Sometimes Magic ran off, sometimes he'd put up with a little browbeating and give Purrkins a gentle kick in return. When Magic was done playing with Purrkins, he'd thump and run off and, somehow, Purrkins knew not to follow.

Magic also let me know that he didn't like being confined to a cage by biting and clawing at his cage when he was confined. Certain that metal was probably not good for a rabbit's teeth, I left his cage door open so he could run around the bedroom all day and night. The door to the Bunny Bedroom was left closed much of the time, but we did let Purrkins go into the room to play with Magic in the morning, most evenings after work and most of the weekend. The two became good buddies.

In fact, over the course of the next year, the relationship between bunny and kitten matured into that of rabbit and cat. Normally, that wouldn't mean anything, but in my house, it meant Magic's hormones kicked in and he fell in love with Purrkins. I know this because, one day, as

Purrkins sat at my feet to await the swirling of the flushing toilet water, Magic appeared from the Bunny Bedroom, and, seconds later, was vibrating his mid-section against Purrkins. From that point on, whenever Purrkins ran into the bathroom and Magic was running around the house, Magic went after Purrkins, sniffed him, tried to snuggle him, and, often, tried to mate with him.

After seeing our two fuzzy strays going at it, one of Mark's favorite questions to me was whether I wanted to play "The Purrkins and Magic Game?" Indeed I would have more often, but my cute little white bunny outfit was really uncomfortable, and the darn ears kept flopping over.

Tip #34: Even an Angel Pup isn't liked by everyone.

While the fall of 2005 brought us a kitten and rabbit that loved each other, October 2006 brought bad tidings in the form of a boxer—the four-legged kind—that attacked Dusty while I was walking him and Little Dipper in a nearby woodlot. The boxer was with its owner, and while the owner's little white Chihuahua-type doggie was on a leash *and* in her arms, she had her boxer at her side and hoped to keep him there with the word, "Stay."

I thought she had a hold of the boxer's collar, but as I walked by with my dogs, the boxer leaped at Dusty. In an instant, Dusty's leash was out of my hand and I shut down, or stepped back away from myself, or had an out-of-body experience, as Dusty rolled and ducked and rolled to get away from the bigger, biting dog. I yelled at the owner to "Get Your Dog The Hell Off Mine!" and could have sung the first verse of George Thoroughgood's "Bad To The Bone" in the time it took the boxer to stop snarling, and for Dusty to stop yelping.

When the dogs were finally separated, I gently pulled Dusty further away from the boxer, and tried to calm him so his yelping subsided to a panicky sound I hadn't heard him make before. My heart was pounding in my chest as I looked him over, but all I saw was a bite wound on his ear. The lady was talking—an apology, I think, something about "never done that before," —but all I heard was Dusty's panicky, almost hyperventilating sound. Singularly focused on getting Dusty and Dipper out of the woodlot and home as fast as I could, I failed to ask the lady for her name or address. It was only a quarter mile walk home but getting there seemed to take an hour.

I gingerly lifted Dusty into the kitchen sink and sprayed and scrubbed his entire body, looking for other wounds in fur as thick as a sheep in desperate need of shearing. I would have had better luck trying to find a flea on a black rabbit.

The next day, I put Mark on an airplane to Denver for some work-related something or other and took the dogs for a walk at Lake Lansing North Park. In less than fifty feet, I realized Dusty wasn't acting his usual peppy self; he was limping along, acting like a dog with no appetite for the fun walk in front of him. Sensing something was wrong, I guided both dogs back to the car. It was while helping Dusty up onto the high seat of my 4Runner that I saw a second bite wound under his shoulder.

The clock in my car said 5:54 and I broke speed records to get to the vet. One car was in the lot. Lights were still on, but a technician had just locked the doors. I knocked vigorously, and when I explained my story to the technician, he contacted the vet, who saw us immediately. She recommended that she shave Dusty to determine how deep the one wound was.

Because Dusty is very sensitive (as we choose not to use the word wimpy), and because I declined to help, the vet took Dusty to the back room to get some help holding him while she shaved him. Before I tuned out and started humming to myself, I heard the vet say something about poking around with a Q-Tip to see how deep the wound was. Even while humming and looking at cute puppies in a Dog Fancy magazine, I heard moaning and a yelp above the electric shaver, which made me wiggle and turn as white as my beleaguered dog.

After an eternity, the vet returned without Dusty and bearing the bad news that she could not tell how deep the wound was. She recommended exploratory surgery. She also warned me that if the wound was such that an organ had been punctured, I'd have to come pick up Dusty immediately and take him to the Michigan State University Small Animal Clinic for additional emergency surgery, because that was out of the scope of her expertise.

Suddenly, I was alone with Mark's beloved, severely injured dog and Mark was nowhere to be reached. If I allowed the surgery and the dog Mark always wanted died, I would feel so very bad. If I didn't allow the surgery and the dog Mark always wanted died of an infection, I would feel so very bad. If the vet found really serious wounds, I'd have to take the dog Mark had always wanted to the MSU Vet clinic for even more surgery that might kill the dog Mark always wanted. And I would feel so very bad.

Since it seemed like I would feel so very bad no matter what, I used my dial-a-friend option, polled an audience of one, did the 50:50 option and finally gave the vet my final answer. I went home feeling sick and helplessly frustrated.

I did my best imitation of a nervous wreck as Dusty underwent extensive surgery to determine the depth of the wounds. While I drank a beer or four, the vet shaved Dusty and followed a line of bruising along Dusty's entire left side.

There, she found another bite wound deeper than the first near his back left leg. She called me after the surgery, saying that both wounds were long but not deep, that she had inserted a few drainage tubes in him, and I could probably get him late the next day. With time on my hands and only one dog, a kitten, two guinea pigs, a rabbit and several mice to attend to, I got online and found the number for Mark's motel. I left a pathetic message on his answering machine, letting him know what had transpired and hoping that I had done okay.

I did my best taking care of all my charges that first night alone, except that I forgot to feed the fish. There were about 40 of them in a 90 gallon tank Mark had purchased for himself on Valentine's Day a couple of years prior when the 55 gallon tank donated by a friend had leaked all over the floor. For the second time. The 40 fish ranged from the common neon tetra to an elephant nose we called Nose, all of whom went hungry the first night under my care. If they'd splashed around in the tank and looked hungry, I might have noticed. But fish just aren't very communicative.

The next day I spent some very unfocused hours at work and couldn't wait to pick up Dusty. I left early and at 4:00, I led a very wobbly-legged Dusty to the car and, mumbling under my breath, tried to figure out how to hoist up a 30-pound, doped up dog with 4 drainage tubes hanging down from his stomach. I lifted him under his rear and chest, placed him gently on the floor and drove slowly home. He moaned the whole time.

At home, I carefully lifted Dusty from the car, and watched him wobble around the yard to relieve himself with an exceptional moan. He paused at the front steps, so I put one hand on his left shoulder and my other hand on his right hip and helped him maneuver up the steps. I opened the door, helped him up the last step and watched him amble down the hall to a bedroom I had lined with towels. He moaned as he gingerly lowered himself down on the towels, and when I saw the pain in his eyes, my heart ached. I sat with Dusty for two hours, petting him on the head, talking to him, trying to make him comfortable. I told him I was sorry I hadn't been more careful and that Mark would be home in a few days to make him feel better. Mark called that evening telling me he was sorry for Dusty, sorry for my trouble, sorry he wasn't there to be with Dusty and me.

After I hung up the phone, I checked in on Dusty, gave him a pain pill in a small wad of cheese, and made him as comfortable as possible, which means I patted him on his head, looked into his sad eyes and told him he would feel better in the morning. I shut the door behind me and felt horrible leaving him in a room all by himself.

In the morning, I let Dipper outside and checked on Dusty. His tail wagged ever so perceptively and when I patted him on the head he blinked and slowly came out of the fog he was in. After another moment, he struggled to his feet. Wobbly at first, he followed me to the front door and outside. I stood in the doorway, watching my dogs, the one looking so tiny with her partner, the other looking nothing like the fluffy watch dog he used to be.

Dusty followed me back to the bedroom, waited for me to put down clean towels and licked my hand when I kneeled down to pet him. His eyes were still cloudy, he was still in pain, but his wounds were oozing and healing. It was the best we could hope for.

When Mark returned the next day, I warned him what his pal looked like and held my breath as he went to the bedroom to see how he was doing. The "ooh" and "poor Dusty" was enough to break my heart.

Mark came out of the bedroom listing several ways he might kill the owner of the boxer, my least favorite of which involved purchasing several poisonous snakes and sneaking into her apartment with them. I told him that I not only didn't do poisonous snakes, I didn't do visitations to prisons, and suggested that he focus his energy on taking care of Dusty. I also told him I'd try to find the owner of the dog when Dusty was better.

A week or so later, when Dusty's drainage tubes had to come out, Mark was once again busy with a work-related something or other, so it was up to me to take Dusty to the vet. I put a few doggie downers in some pieces of cheese for Dusty, contemplated eating one myself, and an hour later, lifted Dusty in the car and took him to the vet. When the vet came in, she asked if I was willing to hold on to Dusty. I said I was if she'd do it on the floor and so that I could not watch. She agreed. Now, I won't describe what it was like having the first drainage tube removed, but after the second one, I'm quite certain I was as white as Dusty even though I wasn't watching. The vet finished her work and I hastily led Dusty outside, saying I wanted to get Dusty safely tucked into the car before paying the bill. In fact, without fresh air hitting me smack in the face, I would have become one with the ceramic tiles on the floor.

Mark did take Dusty to get his stitches removed because I made sure *I* was busy for that appointment. Within eight weeks, Dusty looked like a sheep in need of sheering on three-fourths of his body. Within 12 weeks, Dusty was pretty much back to his "old pups self," as Mark says.

With free time again on my hands, I went on a stake-out to find the owner of the boxer. I hunkered down in my car like they do on TV, near the apartments where I suspected the offending dog's owner lived. During my second stake-out, I saw the lady walking the dog unleashed again. I took a deep breath, marched across the grass, reintroduced myself and handed her a letter describing the county's leash law and asking for her to pay the vet bill. I turned, marched back to my car and twitched nervously all the way home.

A few weeks later, she appeared at my door, went on tearfully about how sorry she was, asked how Dusty was and—after handing me an envelope with some money— asked if this would be enough to help cover the vet bill. I thanked her, asked her to keep her dog on a leash in the future, and shooed her out of the yard. I stood stoically in my yard unsmiling as she drove away in her late-model SUV. Only when it was out of sight did I finally let my tears fall.

Tip #35: Pets—and pet-loving spouses—can be expensive.

Mark continued to provide more distractions for me, including four more ferrets starting in May 2006. Peanut was a Chunky look-alike that was chubby and loved to play. His favorite thing to do was to roll over onto his back and lie on the floor until somebody tickled his tummy. Hoppie, a brown Rocky look-alike without a mean thought in his entire skinny body, loved to leap from the cedar chest into the linen closet where he rooted around in the towels. Smiggles was a white female with a paintbrush stroke of gray on her head and down her back. She was named while Elizabeth and I were under the influence of fumes while hand-painting the Bunny Bedroom. Elizabeth said something about the way the white ferret smiles and wiggles, then said the word smiggles, and that was that. The fourth ferret, Chip, was a small sable female with a white patch on her face and feet and enough energy to wear out all three of her buddies.

By the time the second batch of ferrets came into my life, Elizabeth was a junior in high school and living with us. Strangely, she was unwilling to share her room with the ferrets, so they had to share the Bunny Bedroom with Magic. Since ferrets in the wild eat rabbits, this made things a bit complicated. Not to mention that Magic doesn't like being in a cage.

Our routine with the rabbit, cat, ferrets and dogs was to: let the dogs out in the morning; open the door to the Bunny Bedroom so Magic could greet Purrkins; bring the dogs inside; close the bedroom doors; clap our hands for Magic to jump into his cage; let the ferrets out and fling a towel over the side of the tub so they could get a drink of water from a dish; do poop patrol; wash our hands and give out a few treats; get the ferrets back to their cage; open Magic's cage door so he could run about the bedroom; shut back bedroom doors; feed Purrkins, the pigs, mice and gerbils and turn on the light over the aquarium; spread corn, peanuts and sunflower seeds around outside for the outside animals; pat Dusty and Little Dipper on the head and give a treat; check to make sure we know Purrkins isn't locked in a bedroom somewhere; leave for work hopeful that the shoes and socks we have on match whatever fur-covered clothes we're wearing.

By the winter of 2006, Purrkins discovered a sewing needle and thread that Elizabeth had left on the kitchen table, and managed to get the needle embedded in the roof of his mouth. While at the vet for that wee operation, Purrkins was diagnosed with tapeworms, which not only added to the expense of the vet visit, it got me worrying about what other animals had tapeworms. Mark must have known my parasitic nightmares returned in full, because while I was lying in bed one night, Mark did this hand-wiggle on my leg to imitate a tapeworm.

In case Magic was the source of the tapeworms, I took Magic to a small animal vet in February 2007, and learned that rabbits only pass on tapeworms if they, the rabbits, are eaten. That was the good news. The bad news was that I also was told that Magic had overgrown teeth and possibly a deformed jaw. The vet also convinced me Magic might spend less time pooping all over the bedroom if he weren't a true male wanting to mark his territory. So, in addition to some dental work, I decided to have Magic neutered.

I dropped Magic off on a Friday morning and called twice that afternoon to see how he was doing. Both times, I got this odd feeling all was not quite right with my little bunny. I went to see the vet at 6:15 that evening and at 6:45 the vet finally brought Magic out and told me that he had almost died on the operating table. The vet explained that cats are notorious for taking deep breaths and suddenly exhaling during an operation, but this was the first time she'd had a rabbit under anesthesia that took a deep breath. When he didn't start breathing right away, she put a tube down his throat and started doing compressions on his chest. While Magic did finally start breathing again, he had turned color (she didn't say which color but since he's all white . . .), and gave her quite a scare.

The vet went on to show me X-rays of normal rabbit teeth in a book, followed by Magic's X-rays before and after the surgery, at which point I started feeling queasy. Magic's "before" X-rays showed teeth that had been broken off and regrown, and others with roots that hadn't grown back into the jaw as far as they should. "It was amazing Magic was eating at all," the vet said. She showed me the "after" X-rays again and I think I must have turned white as Magic, because she asked me if I was all right.

After that, I think I checked out mentally. I remember

cramming a small, brown bottle and syringe into my pocket and, as we mechanically went through the motion of putting Magic into the carry-cage and reassembling all the little nuts and bolts that held it together, the vet said something about feeding him baby food and making sure he got the antibiotic to fight the infection in his mouth. When she placed Magic in the cage, all I could see were his black eyes rolling to the back of his head, as if he was not certain this life was better than the hereafter.

Over $300 later, I took my raspy-breathed rabbit back home, tears welling in my eyes. Mark saw my look, stood and followed me to the bedroom with, "Get a towel, we'll need to try to keep him warm."

As I wandered, feeling lost, to find a towel, the phone rang. The vet was on the other line, apologizing for not being more specific about the type of baby food Magic needed. She clarified that Gerber applesauce with rice was what we needed, and to break that up, we could try mixing canned pumpkin with some Ensure. "Try to get three syringes of food in him, once every hour before you go to sleep, and every hour during the day tomorrow. In the meantime, try to keep him warm."

It was the first of four times she would call with advice or to check on Magic.

Mark covered Magic up with a towel and we went to the store and returned with two jars of baby food, some Ensure and a small can of pumpkin. We gave Magic an hour alone before we approached with our tiny syringe and jar of baby food. He made no attempt to get away, no attempt to open his mouth, no attempt to do anything but breathe in that Darth Vader raspy breath.

"At least he'll finally let us pet him," Mark offered.

He lifted Magic's head with one hand and, ignoring the

whimpering noise and the really fast breathing, gently stuck the syringe into Magic's sore mouth. At first, all the food dribbled out, but after Magic realized we were serious, he made a sucking noise and ate. I filled the syringe again with baby food and Mark fed him some more. After three syringes, Magic's face was a mess, his eyes still looking like they wanted to roll backwards forever, and his breathing was downright scary.

"I hope he makes it," was all Mark said as he tucked a towel around Magic before we left the room.

We force-fed Magic three more times that night. First thing in the morning, Mark went in and checked on Magic and informed me he was still alive. We fed Magic a dozen times throughout the day, none more productive or inspiring than the one before. When the vet called wanting to know how Magic was doing, I said he was still holding his own and asked how long we'd have to force him to eat. She said he probably had quite a sore mouth and that if we didn't get that food in him we'd need to take him in for a shot of Vitamin B.

Between the first visit and the surgery, I'd spent $357 on a rabbit that Mark and I had spent three evenings at Rose Lake trying to catch. I wasn't about to spend another wad of money on a Vitamin B shot because we failed to get food into this rabbit. As with Chunky, the force-feeding was hard for me. But Mark had rescued and helped many an animal. At one time, he had a graceful chameleon who, when she was quite old, hyperextended her tongue. Mark found her in her cage with her tongue straight out and stuck on the cage, unable to wind it back into her mouth. Mark moistened her tongue with water and she was able to wind it back into her mouth again. The next day, however, the chameleon's tongue was stuck out again, and had been thusly for so long that the tongue itself—the tissue—was dead. Mark cut off the tongue, put antibiotic on the little stump and fed his chameleon crickets by hand for the rest of her little life.

So for Mark, taking care of Magic was no big deal.

For me, it was something to obsess about. I thought perhaps Magic might start getting tired of having the baby food crammed down his mouth, so I took some of the canned pumpkin and spooned some into a bowl. To this, I added some strawberry Ensure. It was a horrifying mixture, not unlike something that I'd seen erupted from Conrad when he was sick. I flushed it down the drain without even offering it to Magic, along with the rest of the can of pumpkin and the rest of the bottle of Ensure. I offered the remaining three bottles of Ensure to a friend preparing for a colonoscopy.

On Sunday, two days after his operation, Magic picked up a raisin I had bitten in half, rolled it around in his mouth, and spit it back out. He hopped off under an overturned dog bed to hide from "Team Syringe." We were on him in a flash, crammed five syringes of food into him, and were out of the room in less than three minutes.

On Monday, Magic finally ate a couple of raisins. Within a week, he was back to eating his rabbit pellets and fully recovered, pooping hither and yon around the room and trying to hump Purrkins. In three weeks, his attraction to Purrkins subsided and he also began to religiously use the new gigantic plastic poop pan I purchased just for him.

Tip #36: Sometimes it's handy not having cash in one's wallet.

Coinciding nicely with Magic's recovery was the Agriculture and Natural Resources Week at Michigan State University, part of which included an annual rabbit and guinea pig show. As soon as Mark realized Magic was going to recover, he mentioned the show and the fact that he'd always wanted a lion head bunny, and could we maybe go to the show? So, with my mom along, we drove to the show, only to see over two dozen horse trailers in the parking lot. I turned into an overflow parking lot, laughing out loud at the sign in front of the pavilion announcing a horse show in progress. Poor Mark was so excited about the rabbit show he'd gotten us there a week early. While my mom and I laughed, Mark pouted in silence.

A week later, we returned for the actual rabbit show, where there were rabbits instead of horses. As Mark's luck would have it, the very first cage he saw held several lion head rabbits. Admittedly, they were quite cute, but with a $357 bill to pay for Magic, and having paid for Purrkins' needle extraction before that, I wasn't terribly excited about another pet. Mark had that look of "I want" in his eyes, and even went so far as to check his wallet to see if he had the $15 the sellers were asking for the lion head. He had $8 and change. He shook his head and joined my mother and me to look at the other hundreds upon hundreds of other rabbits. Among them were these three-foot-long, reddish-tan rabbits with giant dewlaps drooping under their chins. They were sprawled out on the bottom of their cages, their ears flopping to their sides. Mark asked me if I wanted one. I told him I couldn't imagine the amount of rabbit poop I'd end up cleaning up, and, no, thank you.

An hour later, after finding only two hot-tots like Magic—neither of which had bad teeth—we headed back to the entrance. As my mother and I moseyed slowly away, Mark stopped for one more look at the lion head. When he finally caught up with us, he frowned kind of funny and said, "You know, I said I really wanted to see a lion head. It was amazing that a lion head was the first rabbit that I saw at the show. But maybe you're right. We have enough animals for now."

"Thanks, honey," I said, patting him on the back.

"Maybe next year," he said.

Only time would tell if he could wait that long for something else he'd always wanted.

Or for something else to come into our life that we didn't know we'd always wanted.

Tip #37: A domestic duck can have as much personality as a dog.

CHAPTER 7

Bumpkin

Mama Gerbil died in mid-March 2007. I found her looking not unlike roadkill, lying on her side, her stiff legs sticking straight out of one of the tubes in her cage. Because her body was just inside the plastic tube that led to the top of the cage where the three ladies pooped, her black and white daughter got stuck in the top of the cage all night without food or water.

Mama Gerbil's tan daughter died within a week. Mark's favorite mouse—whom Conrad had named Cinderella—wrinkled his face for the last time in March as well. The remaining gerbils and mice were all off to rodent heaven shortly thereafter.

By 2007, word about the number and kinds of critters Mark and I had raised had spread far and wide, or at least among my co-workers. One co-worker was a bright-eyed and very smart student aide by the name of Nicole. In fact, Nicole was smarter than me, because she only stayed with state government long enough to graduate from college and head to eye doctor school in Chicago.

It just happened that in early April 2007, Nicole was still in East Lansing and attending Michigan State University when she discovered a duckling in somebody's yard, just wandering around. Nicole knew that the duckling would not survive in the "wilds" of East Lansing on its own, so nabbed the duck and asked if I could provide it a more permanent home. Without hesitation, I said, "Sure."

I had no idea what kind of baby duck Nicole was bringing me, and when I sat back and became momentarily logical, it occurred to me that I really didn't know anything about ducks except that they, like all creatures, need food, water and shelter. But I felt that perhaps I had a leg up on raising ducks by having watched dozens upon dozens of mallards in my back yard. Besides, how hard could it be to raise a baby duck?

Mark was excited about the prospect of raising a baby duck, because he'd had one for a brief time when he was a child. And all he did was provide it with food, water and shelter. Perfect!

I also had going for me the fact that in Mark's former life—on 10 acres of land with four children and a lawyer for a wife—he had raised turkeys from eggs. No record exists as to why Mark went to a place called Van Atta's Greenhouse in the Lansing area one day long, long ago and got himself two baby turkeys that grew up and started dropping eggs. But drop eggs they did, and more the next day, and when all was said and done, they had dropped over 40 eggs, which Mark put in an incubator and raised. The story is that the baby turkeys imprinted on Mark and followed him up and down his ½-mile driveway and all around his yard. Mark had such a good time watching those turkeys grow that it wasn't much of a stretch to think that perhaps he was the very guy I needed to help raise a baby duck.

On April 17, 2007, at around 3:00 p.m., Nicole approached me at work with a large shoebox, the contents of which was peeping. Word had gotten out that I was taking possession of a duckling, so with my new charge in hand and a half dozen co-workers gathered 'round, I lifted one corner of the lid. Before I could see inside, the creature pushed upward on the lid of the box, and within seconds, we were face to face with a bright yellow duckling with orange feet and an orange bill. I heard several people say, "Oh, how cute." One person asked, "What are you going to do with it?" but all I could do is wonder, "*What kind of duck is this?*" My next thought was that the little duckling would jump out of the box, so I had no choice but to replace the lid and carry my peeping charge out of the building and to my car.

Because the height of the box was only half the height of the duckling, I couldn't bear to keep the duckling inside the box if I didn't have to. Once I was seated inside my car and the door closed, I lifted the lid, took the duckling in my left hand and held it against my chest. It blinked, looked around, but made no attempt to wiggle or get away. So, using one hand to hold my duckling and the other to drive, we made our way the 10 miles home. The duckling never did wiggle; it was as if sitting on my chest was his or her preferred method of travel.

As we drove through the streets of Lansing, East Lansing and into Haslett, I was amazed by the heat coming off its little feet. Duck feet look rubbery, so I wasn't expecting them to warm my chest. And when we took the turn into my neighborhood and I held the duckling close to my face, I wasn't expecting its beak to be warm, too.

Once safely home, I carried the duckling inside where we were greeted by two curious dogs and one meowing kitten. The duckling blinked and peeped once in response. I told the three curious fuzzies that this was our new pal, and they would have to get used to it being around.

I carried the duckling down to the bathroom and placed her in a cardboard box I had retrieved from the local grocery store the day before. The box was lined with newspapers and soft towels, the former to throw out each day, the latter because a nest would likely have been soft and fuzzy, or at least not hard, I was thinking, and, well, okay, it was totally irrational to put towels in there, but I did anyway.

Above the box was a trouble light, which provided the primary source of warmth for the little duckling. The proper height of the light was very important—if it was too close to the bottom of the box, the duckling would bake; too far away and it wouldn't be able to stay warm enough. What constituted too far and too close was completely beyond me and I had to trust that Mark would adjust it based on the fact that he had not baked any of his baby turkeys.

Everything looked to be in order, less the matter of food, and I was contemplating my next move when Mark appeared. Looking at the duckling he remarked, "Oh my, what a cutie. Do you know what kind?"

"I haven't a clue."

We stood there and stared at the duckling, who stared back at us, blinking every now and again. Finally, it peeped. Mark began talking to it, introducing himself and telling the duckling it had fallen into good hands. He picked it up and the duckling stopped peeping. As he was babbling on to the happy little duckling I asked, "So, uh, what do baby ducks eat?"

"Duck starter," he said, and he turned as if snapping out a trance. "They'll have it at Soldan's."

Since Mark had immediately assumed the role of the alpha male duck, I assumed the role of the alpha female duck, meaning, while he took up vigilance of the duckling, I found myself driving the fifteen minutes or so to a pet store in search of something I didn't know existed. As I drove, I had plenty of time to ponder why anyone had named the substance I was looking for "duck starter." The word "food" worked for just about every other species of animal, and the duckling I was going to feed had already started out in life without the substance I was looking for, so what I really needed was "duck keep growing." On the other hand, I pondered, why isn't human baby food called "kid starter"?

After wondering if anyone else has these types of issues, I asked the Soldan's staff if they had duck starter. I was directed to the back corner of the store where, sure enough, there were five and ten pound bags of this pulverized pale tan-looking stuff labeled so that even I could determine what it was. The store also had turkey starter, which is probably how Mark's turkeys had started out and why Mark knew duck starter existed.

After I found the duck starter, I wondered what other things I might find in the store for ducks, so I wandered up and down the aisles looking for duck grower, duck finisher, duck preening supplies, duck bathing gels, something else for ducks. I found row after row of stuffed toys and bones and food and kitty litter and even horse supplies, but nothing for ducks. To be sure I hadn't missed something, I asked the clerk at the desk. She was a long-haired brunette with a narrow, horse-like face, a neck like a Rottweiler and a rear end like a hippo.

"Do we have what?"

"Anything for ducks besides duck starter?"

"Like—?" she asked, turning her mane sideways and snorting like a piglet.

"Like, you have all these squeaky toys and beds and bones and everything for dogs, so, what do you have for ducks?"

"Ducks only need food and water and to be kept safe and warm," she said, waving a fat panda-like claw.

"And ducks are different than dogs, then, in what way?"

"Dogs are fuzzy and loyal; ducks are feathery and messy?" she asked, her face wrinkled like a perplexed monkey.

"And that explains why you don't have anything else for them besides duck starter?"

"I guess."

As I drove home with my little bag of food, I couldn't help but count the number of stuffed toys we'd given to my childhood dogs, Candy and Ashley—God rest their souls—the plush beds they didn't use because they'd slept with me, and the rawhide bones that once littered our house. How ridiculously spoiled our beagle and cocker spaniel had been, since all they needed was food and water, safety and warmth. And of course, we'd taken spoiling to a new level with Dusty and Little Dipper.

But rather than pondering the hundreds of dollars wasted on dogs, as I pulled into the driveway with my first of what would be many bags of duck starter, I came to appreciate ducks for their simple needs.

"Have any problems?" Mark asked. He was sitting on the bathroom floor while the duckling was running about, pecking at the newspaper.

"Walked right to it," I smiled.

After tucking the duckling in the box, Mark took the bag and sprinkled some of the powdery stuff on top of the water bowl. This created a circular pattern of spinning tan speckles.

"That's fascinating," I said. I turned my attention to the duckling, who was also watching the water spin around.

"See, ducks are attracted to things that move," Mark explained. "In the real world, it's stuff like bugs and worms. But here, when powdery food is placed on water, it creates movement. The duckling will peck at it, realize its edible, and in no time, start eating the Purina duck starter."

I raised a skeptical eyebrow and waited for Mark to stop adding duck starter to the water, for the water to almost stop moving. I was about to sneer when the duckling stepped up to the bowl, dipped his head in the bowl, mucked up his beak and began to eat. And while it ate, it peeped. It was the cutest thing to hear a duck happily peeping away while eating. At times, it peeped with its head in the food-water mixture and made bubbles.

Convinced that the little duckling would survive we named her Bumpkin.

Tip #38: Dogs and cats can be trained not to eat baby ducks.

With a name bestowed upon our downy pal, and the matters of food, safety and water addressed, we decided to take Bumpkin outside. Since outside is where most ducks live and hang out, I, for one, did not want to deprive my duckling of being as duck-like as possible. The thing was, lying between Bumpkin and the great outdoors was a curious cat and two jealous dogs.

Mark left me and Bumpkin in the bathroom, picked Purrkins up, petted him on the head saying, "Good Kitty," and locked him in Elizabeth's bedroom. Then he knelt down on the floor, took both of the dogs by the collar, and when he yelled, "Okay!" I opened the bathroom door and stepped out. As I walked down the hallway and into the living room, Bumpkin followed, halting only for a moment when the dogs lurched forward. Mark pulled the dogs back with a stern "NO!" Bumpkin turned the corner to the front entryway and followed me outside.

The safest place for keeping an eye—or two—outside is just to the right of our front door, which is actually the left side when facing the house, which is behind you if you have your left side to the front door, and in front of you if you have your right side to the front door. From the outside, of course.

Wherever this place is outside our front door, it's perfect for watching a little duckling because it's enclosed on three sides—by a side of the house, a wall of the garage, and a brick wall that serves no other purpose than to provide a third side to box in ducks. In this six-foot-by-four-foot area, Bumpkin ran around under some lily-of-the-valley and ferns, pecked at the ground, pecked at the plants, and peeped when she lost sight of me in the vegetation. I was always nearby, guarding the open area just outside the door.

With the sun setting on our first partial day together, I opened the door, asked Mark to hold the dogs and when he yelled that it was safe, I opened the door and led Bumpkin inside. Bumpkin followed back down the hall, turned right and followed me into the bathroom.

I was about to put her into her box for the night when one last thing occurred to me: ducks like water. And maybe they like water because it does something to their feathers. Or maybe they just like being clean. So perhaps Bumpkin needed a bath. I filled the sink up and lifted Bumpkin in. She stood, flapped her little wing nubbins and splashed around. When she seemed to tire of splashing about, I lifted her down into her box, where she preened for several minutes before lying down on the soft towel under the artificial sun. I was amazed that she'd hatched already knowing about the benefits of duck starter and how to preen.

As her eyes grew heavy under the warmth, she closed her eyes, tucked her tiny beak under her down fuzz, and, peeping quietly, fell asleep.

With Bumpkin tucked safely away, we let Purrkins back out into the main room with the dogs, and played with the ferrets. Our routine was more complicated than ever before, but something about this little duck told me it would be worth it.

Tip #39: A domestic duck may change your life more than you intended.

While Mark and I enjoyed having a baby duck, Dusty did not, because it made his job of guarding us a very difficult one indeed. Dusty's usual modus operandi was to run into the bathroom the moment he returned from the great outdoors, having relieved himself and made sure the neighborhood was safe. After seeking the assistance of a bright fuzzy toy, he'd sit down in the bathroom and guard while Mark and I went through our usual routine. Dusty would leave the bathroom as soon as Mark and I left, and amble out into the main part of the house to guard us from there.

With Bumpkin in the bathroom, Dusty was shut out of the back bedroom area and, instead, sat with his toy just outside the door and whined. Scolding him for whining caused every last bit of fur on his fuzzy face to go flat and lifeless, which made us feel horribly guilty since he was just trying to carry out his self-assigned duties. So instead of scolding any further, we went about our routine ignoring the whining pup on the other side of the door and moving him out of the way when it was time to take Bumpkin outside.

Dusty's reward for putting up with the duckling was sleeping in the bed with Mark and me because of my paranoia.

See, if the dogs were to sleep in the tiny hallway-alcove area where the three bedrooms and bathroom join, Bumpkin was only one door away. I didn't like betting against the extraordinary odds that the dogs could figure out how to open the door, chase Bumpkin into a corner and eat her at 3 a.m. while Mark and I were sleeping. So the dogs came into our bedroom, putting two closed doors—the bedroom door and the bathroom door—between them and Bumpkin. And allowing my overly imaginative mind to sleep.

And yes, Dusty's toys came into bed with him. I can tell you there's nothing like rolling over onto a squeaky toy in the middle of the night, followed by a 30-pound dog loping across the bed to retrieve the toy and make it squeak a few more times before settling down somewhere else. I must say, however, that a squeaky toy is better to roll upon than a rawhide bone.

With Bumpkin in our lives, our morning routine started with Mark rolling over to his left to hit the snooze button on the alarm clock, and rolling back to the right to see which dog had worked its way from the foot of the bed to a place between Mark and me, with its fuzzy little head resting on one of our pillows.

If the dark eyes that met Mark's glance blinked in rhythm to a flapping tail, it was Dusty who had taken over the coveted position at the top of the bed; if the blinky eyes came with a paw to Mark's face followed by a slobbery lick it was Little Dipper. Once the luckier of the two dogs reminded Mark it was time to get up—or by the third hit of the snooze button, whichever came first—Mark would let the two dogs out the front door, while I showered. After drying off, I'd fill the sink for Bumpkin and lower her in. As she'd splash about the sink and flap her wing nubbins, I'd clean up after Bumpkin by replacing her towels and newspapers. Meanwhile, Mark would let the dogs in, let the ferrets run around in their bedroom, shave, and get himself ready for work. We'd finish getting ready for work constantly aware of where Bumpkin was in relation to the two dogs, Purrkins and the ferrets. And where the ferrets were in relation to the rabbit. And so on.

Before we'd leave for work, we'd put Bumpkin in her box, shut the door and try hard to ignore the loud peeping of our baby duckling. When we'd come home, we'd let the dogs out the front door on their lines. With the dogs in the front yard, we'd respond to the peeping from the bathroom by either carrying Bumpkin down the stairs to the basement and outside to the backyard, or by holding the dogs and letting Bumpkin walk out the front door and around the side of the house to the backyard.

I loved our walks outside, because there was always a lot going on: birds singing, bugs wiggling and crawling around, squirrels making their way across the street to a tree, to our roof, to the feeders in the backyard. Watching Bumpkin was also fun because she nibbled, prodded and poked everything she saw. Everything was interesting and new. And almost everything made her peep: nibbling on grasses, chasing after bugs, me reaching out and touching her on her beak. If a duck can be happy, Bumpkin was a happy duck.

And while I was generally happy when I was with her, I was always on guard. Melissa's beagles had both slipped their chains before, and it would take but a second for them to be on Bumpkin. Stray cats have hunted in our yard and Bumpkin would be an easy target for them, too. Hawks have also hunted from our trees, so I was on the watch for them as well. I felt completely responsible for my charge as she was completely reliant on me.

And such pressure tends to make me worry. Perhaps obsess.

For example, while watching her dart here and there after bugs, I wasn't sure if I ever really saw her eat any bugs, so I feared she would be protein-deprived if I didn't step in.

Pill bugs are a good source of protein, I reasoned, so I pulled away some of the decayed leaves outside my front door and exposed a dozen or so wiggling pill bugs.

And there we were, me squatting, a few dozen pill bugs running about, and Bumpkin staring at me, her little eyes going blink. Blink. When she didn't make a move toward the wiggling pill bugs, I gently pinched two with the thumb and forefinger of my left hand and waited as they unwound in my right hand. Bumpkin poked at them as if to, well, poke them, and went back to staring at me. Blink. Blink.

Apparently, pill bugs were not on Bumpkin's menu.

Thinking perhaps she preferred worms over pill bugs, I dug around again under the decayed vegetation and pulled out a three-inch long worm. The idea of the tiny duckling eating a worm that, when stretched, was as long as the duckling itself made me gag, but if this is what it took to ensure she had protein—. I held the worm up to Bumpkin. She turned her head sideways, stabbed at the worm, wiped her beak off in the leaves and stared at me. Blink. Blink.

I dropped the worm and am not sure if the sigh I heard was from me, Bumpkin or the worm. As I pondered what to do, I walked slowly along the side yard where we had planted some foot-high grasses that promised to get much taller one day. Bumpkin followed, pecking at the grasses until she'd reached the third plant, at which time she looked up at me and blinked. Wondering if perhaps she was a vegetarian, I continued on to the back yard and under our deck where a half billion seeds and hulls from the bird feeders above had tumbled off the edge of the deck, and where some two-inch high sunflower plants had sprouted. I plucked one easily and held it out for Bumpkin. She snatched it up in her beak and it disappeared.

Thus began our daily search for young sunflower plants

under the deck. Every day, we headed straight for the underside of the deck to pluck sunflower plants, the "we" being me plucking, Bumpkin eating. She never would pluck her own plants—she'd just stand there and stare at me if I stopped pulling them from the ground. Mark said Bumpkin trained me well.

Early on, enough new sunflower seedlings grew overnight to make up for the ones we plucked the day before. But over time, as Bumpkin ate and got bigger, I had to expand my search to under the deck stairs, over by the dogs' kennel, near the hot tub, and inside some plant pots that no longer held any potted plants. I even found some sunflower plants that had sprouted on the deck stairs.

Knowing that Bumpkin would soon out-pace the sunflower plant production, I set about finding other things to attract her attention. I found that she'd nibble on the white fuzzy ends of dandelions, and that if I threw the dandelion greens into her outdoor pool, she'd peck at them and snarf them down.

Perhaps I forgot to mention that every domestic duck needs an outdoor pool? I'd purchased one several years prior when my very young nephew was planning to visit from Illinois. I recall filling up the new green pool several days prior to his visit, and that within hours of the pool appearing in the back yard, adult mallards took it over. Upon seeing this, my bacteria-conscious sister vetoed its use for her son. I kept the pool just in case my sister's daughter might use it one day, which, of course, didn't happen, either. I was only too happy when Bumpkin took to it.

With a pool as part of the picture, our modified routine was to get all the sunflower plants we could find before I picked Bumpkin up, put her in the pool and threw dandelion greens at her. When one of us tired of that, she'd splash about in the pool for a while as I watched her bathe and preen. I loved to watch her preen, partly because I would never do it, and also because there was a sort of ritual to it: she'd dip her head into the water so water would run off her back, splash about the tub by flapping her little wing nubbins, scratch at her head with her feet, and nibble hither and yon with her beak. Then she'd start all over again.

When we tired of the pool, I picked her up, put her on the ground and told her it was time to go inside. She followed me to the basement door and inside the house. I shut the door behind her, she followed me to the bottom of the basement stairs, and I bent down and carried her upstairs. Once upstairs she found a good place to preen. Often, that was under the kitchen table.

Since Bumpkin took to preening without instructions from any other duck, I figured it was a vital duck-like function. Curious about the function preening served, I searched articles online and learned that ducks preen to cover their feathers with oil and make them waterproof. I also learned that bathing helps to clean the feathers of dirt, debris, and external parasites, which is sort of why we clean just about anything, I'd say.

I was only glad Bumpkin had figured out how to preen on her own, because if she *hadn't* figured it out, I'd have had to buy a Big Bird outfit and pretend to preen my feathers and hope she caught on. I could see her staring at me like she does sometimes. Blink. Blink.

Tip #40: The larger the duck, the larger the poo.

It didn't take Bumpkin long to figure out that every time she entered the main open area of our house, she became top dog: The real dogs were warned to behave and Purrkins was removed to a distant bedroom. Because the main part of our house is one big open area, Bumpkin easily navigated her way around and took charge. She ate when she wanted, wherever there was food, and the dogs knew to leave her alone. She also figured out that Mark and I spent most of our time either at our kitchen table plunking away at our computers or reading, so that's where Bumpkin started spending most of her time.

While it was fun to have a fuzzy pal that followed me anywhere, the fact is, she was messy. Ducklings poop wherever they go and apparently don't take to litter boxes like cats and ferret do, or get trained to go outside like dogs. So to keep our carpet from becoming a giant fuzzy litter pan, I spread towels all over the floor.

I even had to spread towels in the kitchen, because Bumpkin showed us that if we failed to put dry duck starter in fresh water, she ate her food by dipping her beak first in the food, then in the water, then back to the food, then to the water. By dripping between the food and water dishes Bumpkin created this tan-brown slurry that, if allowed to dry on the tile floor, turned concrete hard and had to be scraped up with a putty knife. Scraping with putty knives is not on my top-ten list of favorite things to do, so I covered the kitchen floor with towels, too. When a towel was appropriately cruddied up, I took the towel outside and let it dry off on the deck railing. After the towel was dry, I beat it with my hand until all the chunkies fell off and added it to a disgusting pile of other yucked up towels. Meanwhile, a new towel was placed on the floor and the cycle started all over again.

Once a week, I gathered up all the yucked up towels, and while Bumpkin was either confined to the bathroom or outside with Mark, I did laundry. When all the towels were dry,

I spread them on the floor and we started all over again. I also vacuumed once a week to pick up what escaped between the towels. I must share that trying to vacuum downy fuzz—which tends to float in the air—is an unheralded sport. As I vacuumed, the fuzz would rise into the air and to nab it, I'd have to detach the hose and suck it from the air. It's great fun if you have nothing better to do.

Indeed, Bumpkin was a lot of work but worth it because Bumpkin became our pal. She liked to be wherever we were. She hung out wherever Mark and I happened to be and seemed to enjoy settling down on Mark's chest to watch TV on the couch. She'd make this quiet happy peeping sound as she pecked lightly at Mark's fuzzy beard and usually, a few moments later, settle down for a little nap.

Even with Bumpkin in the house, Dusty went about the usual business of sitting on the bolster facing the door so he could watch for bad guys. Little Dipper—the huntress and snuggler—had a harder time. She'd curl up at the far end of the couch and, in a series of extremely subtle moves, use her front legs to wiggle her way up closer and closer to Mark. Once she'd made her way forward enough that her fuzzy little head was within a few feet of the duckling, I gently grabbed Little Dipper and pulled her further away. Over time, she crept forward and repeated the process all over again.

Now, you have to understand that prior to Bumpkin's arrival, Dipper spent most of her nights being petted by Mark or sleeping under a wad of pillows on the couch, so being displaced from either of those luxuries was perhaps a lot to expect from her. Come 10 o'clock or so, when we carried Bumpkin back to her box and tucked her safely away, Little Dipper got our full attention and was petted until her fur almost fell off. So for the last hour of the day anyway, all was well again with the spoiled dogs.

**Tip #41: A duck will bathe in just about any-
thing that holds water.**

By May 4, Bumpkin had eaten up the duck starter and had
worked her way up to the small, skinny pellets called duck
grower. As with the duck starter, she took some of the duck
grower, dipped it in water and slurped. Back and forth she
went, making this slurry of food. Thing is, if the slurry of
yuck sat for more than 24 hours she wouldn't eat it. So every day we dumped out the slurry, gave her fresh water and
food, and she started all over again, making a big mess. She
also liked to eat the dogs' Beneful.

Bumpkin ate and kept eating. In early May she was too
big to float in the bathroom sink, so we lifted her into the
kitchen sink for her bath. That was really handy because after
Bumpkin made a big mess on the floor eating her food or the
dogs' food, we could lift her up and watch her take her bath
while we picked up after her. When she was done with her
bath, we put her on the floor to dry herself off. Then she'd
wander into the living room and watch some TV, sometimes
on the floor, sometimes sitting on Mark's chest.

Every day we went outside at least twice to get fresh air,
and to look for sunflower plants and weeds. The first time it
rained enough for water to pool in small puddles in our
yard, Bumpkin peeped and peeped as she slurped and
sieved through the water. I loved the sound of what I can
only describe as happy peeping noises.

By the third week in May, Bumpkin had outgrown the
kitchen sink and took her baths in the bathroom tub. I
looked forward to these tub trips, because I could close the
bathroom door and read some old newspapers while
Bumpkin splashed around. It was like having a time-out
without getting into trouble first. It was amazing to read

what had gone on in the world when I wasn't paying attention, which, I'm sure you've gathered, is most of the time.

As Bumpkin grew, her confidence in the water also grew. The casual dunking in the water became faster and faster, and was sometimes followed by almost cartoonish runs across the water. Sometimes she got so caught up in dunking and running, she'd suddenly propel herself around in circles. My absolute favorite was when she suddenly dove and swam underwater, because she looked so surprised when she surfaced again. Then she'd do it again and seem amazed all over again.

After a couple of nights watching her do the same things over and over again, I was confident that she'd survive a half hour in the tub without me and left her alone. I migrated to my computer to jot down a few notes while she splashed about. When tub time was over, I put Bumpkin on the floor and watched as she preened herself, flicking the water droplets everywhere.

And that gave me a great idea.

One night, after Mark was lying horizontal on the couch in front of the TV, I took the dripping wet duckling, plopped a towel on Mark's chest like I always did and walked away. I had just pulled the plug on the bathtub when I heard the "Oh, geez!" followed by, "You did that on purpose!"

"What, honey?"

"You brought the wet duck out here and let her spray herself all over me."

"Oh, honey, she's just a tiny duckling. How much water can she really hold on her tiny feathers?"

"Apparently, a lot."

Mark looked pretty funny with a towel pulled over his head, peeking out occasionally while Bumpkin finished preening. When Bumpkin was done preening and had settled down on his chest, I could see by the look in his eye that Mark had also fallen for Bumpkin.

Tip #42: The term "pecking order" is taken pretty literally by a duck.

By the time Bumpkin had converted about half of her fuzzy down to white feathers, the dogs had gotten used to her being in the house and ignored her when she walked by. In fact, if they didn't ignore her, Bumpkin sometimes pecked at them. Purrkins was also allowed to wander in Bumpkin's presence, though we watched her closely, always ready for a hiss and pounce. On occasion, Bumpkin would walk right up to Purrkins as if to say hello, and I often wondered if Bumpkin sensed Purrkins had no front claws. Or if, perhaps, she just wasn't the smartest duck on the block.

While Bumpkin was at the top of the pecking order inside the house, outside, I was still worried about dogs, cats and hawks. It was Bumpkin, though, that clued *me* into a hawk overhead one day when she stopped in her tracks, cranked her head so one eye was straight up in the air, and then ran between my legs. I looked up, saw the Cooper's hawk, waved my arms and yelled at it to go away. It flew off.

One afternoon in the backyard, we loitered long enough for two mallards to wander into the yard in search of corn. Bumpkin looked up from chewing on a sunflower seed, looked at the mallards and, without pause, returned to eating. The mallards often came in quacking, and out of habit I'd quack back at them, but Bumpkin paid them no attention at all.

It occurred to me that Bumpkin's world revolved around us. And surely, our world revolved around her.

But I didn't want to think about that too hard, and after our outdoor adventure we went inside for a bath. This was followed by a nap, which was one of my favorite times, because Mark, Dipper and I would lie on the couch, Dusty on the bolster, and—now that she was older—Bumpkin on the floor right where the bolster and couch met. She'd preen for a while, usually peeping as she did so, then she'd slowly settle down for a nap, tucking her beak under her wing, one eye open at first, and peeping quietly. I'd peep back for a while to let her know her world was safe, and after a few minutes, her eyes would get heavy and close. She'd continue peeping with her beak under her wings for several more minutes before she finally fell asleep; the muffled peeping making me smile. When Bumpkin woke, she'd start peeping quietly again the second she made eye contact with one of us. Mark and I agreed that that sound was one reason why we fell so hard for the little duckling.

The thing about routines, though, is that they become so normal and work so well until someone questions them. Like when my mother stopped by to see Bumpkin, held her, watched her eat, and asked ridiculous questions like, "How logical is this whole set-up? And what are you going to do with Bumpkin when she is fully fledged?"

I remembering looking at my mother and going, "Wha...?" and then looking around at the feathery shaft-bits scattered hither and yon throughout the house, and the tiny feathers that rose from the floor when someone walked by . . . and the towels that I'd just washed and dried and spread around because my mother was coming over, and the mess already in progress in the kitchen where Bumpkin was happily slurping up food and water. I looked at Bumpkin's feathers and how they were overpowering her downy fuzz. And I stood back and kind of saw where my mother was coming from.

But the moment didn't last long and, not knowing what to say, I shooed my mother away and told her she needed therapy because she didn't know what was normal.

See, from our perspective, things were going well for Bumpkin: She was getting her fill of sunflower plants, duck grower and oyster quackers—I mean crackers. She splashed about in the bath tub every day and her efforts to preen seemed to be resulting in a lot of beautiful, white feathers. And she was making a peep-quack kind of noise that was quickly becoming more quack than peep.

So I suppose the signs were there and my mother's visit simply watered a seed that had germinated but been ignored, the message being: "Bumpkin is getting big." I began to enjoy the present less and became bothered by the future. It had made sense to keep Bumpkin safe inside our house, but having a full grown duck in the house didn't seem logical at all. Within a couple of weeks she would turn into a mature duck. A sizeable, white duck. A pekin. Like the Aflac duck. We love the Aflac duck.

The other seed that was planted in my brain was the fact that I was getting tired of replacing and cleaning towels and replacing newspapers every day. With one bum knee, Mark just wasn't able to help out, and I began to question how long I was really willing to go on doing this. I also knew that Bumpkin wasn't suited to spend time outside by herself. She had no defense mechanism and, unlike the mallards that frequented the yard, she seemed very heavy in body and unlikely to be able to fly away from a predator.

As a result of my mother's observations, I realized that our days with Bumpkin were coming to an end, and that we would have to find her a permanent home. When I finally broached the subject with Mark, he frowned, put his head down and nodded in agreement. We made two goals for ourselves: one, make a video tape of our life with Bumpkin; and two, start searching for the best possible permanent home.

That night, Mark picked Bumpkin up, held her close and spoke softly to her as he carried her down to the bathroom for the night.

Tip #43: Domestic ducks were bred to be eaten, which is why most cannot fly.

The reason I know domestic ducks can't fly worth a darn is because in the winter of 2005, two Rouen ducks (which are like mallards on steroids) and a Pekin duck appeared in our backyard and hung out with the mallards for a couple of days. On the third day, I saw them all huddled against our back door and when I looked outside, a hawk was sitting on a tree overhead. I chased the hawk away and made a pile of corn, knowing that was all I could do for the ducks. Two days later, I found the head of the Pekin near the island on our lake. I never saw the Rouen ducks again.

We had to find a home for Bumpkin that provided safety from predators.

Mark called a few local animal rescue places, but none took domestic ducks. One place recommended we call a gentleman who had released other domestic ducks on the pond in his backyard. We drove 20 miles to discover that the pond was a big detention basin that abutted a half dozen other houses. The man claimed previous other charges all flew away, but we suspected instead they went the way of the headless duck.

While Mark was calling zoos in the chance one would take Bumpkin in, I remembered that a few years prior, a coworker had given me the book *Enslaved By Ducks*, by Bob Tarte. It occurred to me that there may be a no more perfect person to harbor our Bumpkin than Bob Tarte. He wrote about pekin ducks and he seemed to love them as much as we did Bumpkin. And I recalled that he was also a Michigander.

I pulled the book out and, sure enough, in the first page, he described the farm-like setting in Lowell, Michigan, an hour or so away. I typed his name on the Internet and found his web site and email address. I wrote him and explained how we had come upon Bumpkin, what she meant to us, and asked if he might possibly consider taking her in. He wrote back almost immediately and agreed, asking only that we bring some duck feed with us.

Almost at the same time, Mark heard back from Deer Forest Fun Park in the southwest part of the state, home of one of the USA's largest petting zoos. We debated where to take Bumpkin. We didn't pet Bumpkin, and the idea of a bunch of strangers petting her bothered me. What if she didn't like being petted? What would they do with Bumpkin if it didn't work out? On the other hand, what if Bumpkin didn't get along with Bob Tarte's other ducks?

We decided on the Tartes and sent a $100 donation to Deer Forest Fun Park and thanked them for their willingness to take our duck.

From that point forward, time went quickly. We made our Duckumentary on May 25 showing Bumpkin emerging from the bathroom, walking down the hall, taking a left and walking out the front door. From there, she walks along the side of the house, gets sunflower seeds and plays in her pool. The brief video captures a typical day in the life of Bumpkin.

The days between then and June 1 were as sweet as the others, but always weighing on us was the knowledge that we were running out of time with our pal, Bumpkin.

Tip #44: Saying good-bye isn't easy, even to the face of a duck.

173

June 1, 2007, started like any other day, only everything we did was being done for the last time: the last time Bumpkin would walk past the dogs and the cat and out the front door; the last time I would feed Bumpkin sunflower seeds, watch her take her bath and preen; the last hug I would give her. I found myself chattering to her as Mark held her closely and carried her out to my Honda Element, lowered her gently inside and explained that we were going on a road trip and that she would soon be making new friends.

For the hour-long ride, Bumpkin laid down in the slot between the two front bucket seats. We chatted, she'd peep-quack back, and it was like the first day and as if she had always gone traveling in a car. We arrived at the Tarte's before noon and Linda Tarte came out to meet us, her long hair in a braid, her eyes warm and welcoming. Bob joined us moments later and introduced himself as Mark carried Bumpkin to their big red barn. Attached to the main part of the barn was a large fenced in, covered area with lots of other ducks running around, as well as several chickens. There was also a blue swimming pool.

Mark placed Bumpkin on the ground and she stood nearby as Bob emptied the pool and refilled it. Bumpkin stepped in the pool and took a drink, stepped out and pecked at the first duck that approached her. A chubby chicken approached and she ignored it. I worried that she wouldn't fall in with them, wouldn't accept them or them her. But I also knew we had no other option.

I walked numbly behind Linda and Bob as they took us into their home to chat for a few minutes. I remember little of the visit except that they had a rabbit and several birds and that they let their birds fly about while they made dinner. They were polite and gracious but all I could think about was Bumpkin.

We thanked them for giving Bumpkin what looked like a great home and drove off without a final farewell to our beloved duck. Down the road, Mark said it best when he said, "You were a great little duckling and a beautiful big duck, Bumpkin. And we will miss you."

After wiping away a tear, I added, "And may you fall for a good looking Muscovy, or even a chicken."

At home, I did the final washing of towels, the final scrubbing of floors, and what I mistakenly thought was the final vacuuming of feathery debris. In fact, it would take months before the last of the tiny feathers made their way out of the corners of our house and into the air to get nabbed by the detachable hose. Nabbing those feathers wasn't so much fun anymore.

I think Mark and I were both surprised at the way a little duckling touched us with her trust and simplicity. She followed us everywhere and was a pal and a pet as much as the dogs and cat. Her quiet peeping and quacking was like the purring of our cat, the wagging of the dogs' tails—it was a sign that she was happy. The idea that we couldn't keep her forever tugged at us for a long, long time.

In looking back, it still amazes us how our lives became entwined with a feathery critter for only a few short months and how they were three of the most fulfilling months we've ever had. And it amazes me that my eyes still tear up when I see photos of Bumpkin.

Tip #45: All pets die.

Tip #46: It's always hard when pets die.

CHAPTER 8

A Few Furs out of Place

After raising Bumpkin, we went two years before any new critters came into our home, because without warning, our priorities changed.

In February 2009 we were devastated to learn that my father had mesothelioma, a form of lung cancer caused by exposure to asbestos. This news shook our world not only because most people only live 9-12 months once diagnosed, but also because the doctors knew he had cancer in January 2008 when his lung collapsed, once, twice, three times, and when they did radical surgery, patched him up, and took a sample to pathology. Somehow, the pathology results were never shared with us until February 2009, which is like over a year after the doctors knew.

Such news makes everything special: time with my father, time with my mother, time with Mark, and with other family members. Trips to cancer treatment facilities were turned into day-long events with Mark and my dad's wife, Norma. Plans were made to see movies, go shooting at the indoor shooting range where my father worked, and to eat at IHOP where I tried time and again to get as good as my dad at blowing a straw wrapper across a restaurant table. My sister brought her family in from Illinois over the summer and we had quite the time together just playing with the big kid that was our dad.

Life itself had suddenly become more special, which is why I also found things going on out in the natural world more special. In the spring of 2009, I took the time to stand in my yard and photograph migrating birds and saw several birds that had probably passed through in years past, like a palm warbler and two species of grebe. Given all the miles each migrating bird had traveled and still had yet to travel, I welcomed them and told them to stop by again when they could stay longer.

I also took notice of the signs of spring and the subtle changes each day: the emergence of the chipmunks from hibernation, songbirds calling before the morning light, the return of large flocks of Canada geese, followed closely by the red-wing blackbirds and robins. By late-March, the male gold finches' dull yellow wings had undergone a magical transformation to a brilliant yellow. Everything around me seemed to be its own small miracle in motion, doing what nature had hard-wired it to do to survive.

It was during this sentimental time that I re-focused on writing this book, because my dad had taken in many cats over the years, had a real soft spot for all types of critters and, okay, I had the odd thought that this book might make things better for critters somehow. Now, writing is not usually a group sport, and I can honestly say that my spouse is not helpful. I admittedly ignored Mark a fair amount during the first few months I was focused on writing; nodding as he blabbed on about this and that, asking what I wanted for dinner, and telling me about the TV schedule for the evening.

So when Mark was admitted to the hospital for what he'd thought was a heart attack but was instead a collapsed lung, I thought perhaps he needed some attention and I put my writing aside for a bit.

Within hours, Mark was comfortably numb on morphine and spent the next five days lying around, waiting to see if the hole in his lung would fix itself. I spent my days with him and my evenings caring for what suddenly seemed like an overwhelming number of critters.

Mark's lung did not fix itself any more than my dad's had, so on day six we set off for surgery to fix the hole. It was apparently two-for-one-surgery day at the hospital because the first surgery didn't work, so we had to have a second, more radical surgery (like my dad's). This very long day was followed by the scariest moments of my life: watching Mark gasp for breath between allergy-related coughing spasms. There were times we were both afraid he'd never catch his breath again. Other times I called him a wuss for wanting a full breath of air.

Five days after his surgeries, Mark began huffing and puffing his way to a full recovery. By March he was back to using his elliptical machine without fear of blowing a piece of his lung across the room. And he was able to help out with the critters again, thank goodness.

March was also when my father finished six weeks of radiation treatment, when my mother turned 74, and when Dusty, who'd turned 11 two months before, developed terrible breath and was having difficulty chewing rawhide bones. I remembered when Little Dipper developed bad breath in the summer of 2008, the result of which was the removal of so many bad teeth she was left with just six. Mark and I had put a large deposit on a Canadian fishing trip, so we had to turn to Elizabeth and my mother to take care of our very unhappy little dog. Upon reaching Canada—and before heading into the bush where phones are only used for emergencies—we called and learned that Elizabeth had discovered peanut butter as being the one thing Dipper would lick and the only way they could get little bits of pain pills into her. By the time we returned 10 days later, Little Dipper was eating soft food. Beneful, specifically. The kind that came in a cute container costing $1.65 on sale. I also soon discovered that canned ravioli and macaroni and cheese worked well too and I could buy those on sale for $1 a can.

Anyway, having felt like scum for what Dipper went through, when we discovered Dusty's bad breath, Mark took Dusty to the vet right away and learned that he had at least one cracked tooth. I arrived home from work to find a urine specimen bottle on the kitchen counter not unlike the one humans use, and a small plastic tray with tiny, bumpy depressions on it. The goal, Mark said, was to collect a urine sample from Dusty because the pre-surgery test to analyze Dusty's urine was cheaper and less painful than the pre-surgery blood sample. Tests like these were recommended for old dogs, to, uh, make sure they could pass urine or had blood or could survive surgery or something. Since Dipper's last tooth extraction cost over $600, saving a few bucks on a urine sample seemed reasonable. And how hard could it be?

How hard could it be, indeed. The dogs were immediately suspicious because usually if Mark and I walk the dogs, he takes one dog's leash and I take the other. This time, Mark took hold of both their leashes and headed down the driveway while I followed behind. Mark's job was to walk them to posts and fire hydrants; my job was to swoop down next to Dusty with the plastic tray and stick it under his leg. There's a fire hydrant right across the street from us, and just as Dusty lifted his leg, I put the plastic container under his leg only to have him kick it away. However, when we reached the nearby lamp post, Dusty was less startled and allowed me to hold the tiny tray between his legs long enough to get a few drops of urine. Mark applauded.

So there I was with this little, bumpy tray with drops of urine gathered in tiny pools. And there I was in our neighborhood trying to get the urine dribbles out of the depressions and into a corner of the tray without tilting the tray so far that the droplets all fell out onto the snow. I was cursing the vet for not giving us a tray with a smooth bottom when I finally said to heck with it, turned the tray over quickly and nabbed what I could in the jar, letting the rest color the snow. I sealed the jar and held it up. "We need about six more of these to give them something to test."

We continued on for two neighborhood blocks and made a game of it—Mark awarded points based on the amount of urine I nabbed while I debated the number of points awarded. I got better with each effort, and at one point Mark said I might consider a second career. Before I could respond, he nominated me to drive the sample to the vet before they closed "because otherwise we'll need to refrigerate it and I know you don't want a urine sample in the fridge."

"How about you take the sample in?" I asked.

"But I took Dusty to the vet this morning for his exam, plus we got shots and a heartworm test. And it was scary, wasn't it Dust?"

Five minutes later I handed my prize to the vet assistant, who held the sample up to the light and said, "Good job."

I was so proud.

Two days later, we dropped Dusty off for his tooth extraction and waited nervously for word from the vet about our beloved pup. We'd both recently realized that Dusty had passed middle age and was now in the senior category of pups that may need soft food for the rest of their lives, like Dipper. We had most of the day to worry about Dusty, because vets tend to do teeth cleanings and dental surgeries after all other procedures. It wasn't until 4 p.m. that we heard that Dusty had survived the surgery. The vet assistant said he should be ready when they closed at six.

"At six?" Mark grumbled after he hung up the phone. "My pup has been there since seven o'clock. That's a long day for my boy."

"And a long day for you, Mr. Hungry and Grumpy. Let's eat, take care of the other animals and go pick him up." Mark agreed.

A couple of hours later, Dusty was indeed ready to go, his legs moving on the slippery floor at the vet office but going nowhere, much like a cartoon character. Once on the concrete, he gained enough traction for his wobbly feet. When I opened the door and lifted him in he looked at me with eyes that were far, far away.

It was then that I realized that Dusty's best days were likely behind him. Bichon Frise can live to 15 years or more and Lhasa apsos live 12-18 years, and the lowest number of those years—12—was nine months away from Dusty's current age.

And so on the way home from the vet, I started thinking that these were our better days and that many of our animals were approaching their normal life expectancy: the dogs were both 11; the guinea pigs old; and, while the ferrets were only four, both Smiggles and Chip had lost over half of the hair on their backs, meaning signs of kidney failure and an early trip to heaven. We didn't know how old Magic was. But we did know grim days were ahead.

Because life had become instantly sacred again, we set about spoiling our animals. One Saturday we dropped the dogs off to get trimmed at PetSmart, ran some errands, went home for a bit, ran a few more errands, and then, before retrieving the dogs from the groomers, paid the bill and bought Dusty a new orange stuffed monkey that squeaks. Dusty pranced out of the store with that bright orange monkey hanging from his mouth.

It would be the last good image of the day.

Minutes after returning from Pet Smart with the dogs, Mark went to the back bedroom and yelled my name twice in a sad, scared voice I hadn't heard before, followed by "Oh no!" I ran back to see Magic dead in Mark's arms and a ferret sitting on top of Magic's cage. Three ferrets were asleep in the ferret cage but one—the little, skinny Chip—had gotten out and apparently chased Magic into a panic-induced heart attack. As Mark whooshed by to spare me—to make it such that the last memory I have of Magic was playing with the giant dandelion weeds that we'd picked up from Meijers only an hour before—and as he went outside to bury Magic on the south side of the house, I numbly took Chip, put her in her cage, and latched the bottom latch I had failed to secure earlier in the day.

I fell to the floor and pounded on the ground and yelled "No!" and "How could I have done this to my friend?" I fell apart after that and remember little, except that I cried and left the room and cried more, and that Mark cried with me and gave me a big hug. He said many nice things—that he loved that I had loved Magic so much, that he loved the way Magic had washed his face with the little bowl of fresh water I gave him twice a day. I don't know what else he said, but it was all good and all true about Magic. I could not say a thing.

Later, we went through all the what ifs: if I'd properly

latched the ferret cage, if we'd been home instead of doing stupid errands early on Saturday morning; if we'd just waited to let the ferrets out after we'd come home from all of our errands; if either of us had checked on the ferrets while Magic was playing with the dandelion greens we'd purchased during our first set of errands. Twice we had gone into the bedroom between errands and after we'd put the ferrets away. Twice we had failed to notice the latch on the cage. If only one of the ferrets hadn't chased him around; if only Magic hadn't panicked and had a heart attack.

I stayed on the couch unmoved for hours while Mark sunk himself into a book. Only hunger got me up although I had no appetite and found even crackers had no taste. Not knowing what else to do, I made myself return to what had been called the bunny bedroom, and told myself I would feel better if I started removing little bits and pieces of what was once Magic's domain. I plugged in the vacuum cleaner and did really well for about two minutes, until I got to a piece of very dense scrap carpeting embedded with magic's white fur that the vacuum couldn't suck up.

Mark found me with the vacuum cleaner running but not moving, my pathetic self bent over at the waist and crying uncontrollably. He asked me what had happened and I told him in broken speech, between tears, that I couldn't get the fur off the carpet. He disappeared and returned moments later with a roller brush we'd gotten to remove Purrkins' fur from our living room carpet. On his hands and knees beside me, Mark rolled the fur away. I finished vacuuming as best I could, knowing—as with Bumpkin—that it would be weeks before I found the last of the fur and the last of the tiny round bunny poop.

I did little the rest of the weekend and had no energy to walk the dogs, or do anything with the ferrets, the guinea pig, or the two black and white dumbo mice that had appeared one day on the kitchen counter. I did notice that one of the mice had two small wounds on its back and informed Mark, but part of me didn't care if he did anything about it or not. I was numb, so heavily did I blame myself, so much did I feel I had let my friend down. Mark separated the mice and surrounded them with cereal boxes so Purrkins couldn't get to them.

I dreaded going to work on Monday, because I was afraid I'd see Brenda; I didn't want to tell her, and I was worried I'd fall apart again. She asked me to go to breakfast and I ended up telling her what I'd done. It felt like a confession. She said that I'd done well for Magic, that I'd extended Magic's life by capturing him and bringing him home, and that I'd provided him the best home possible. It took all I had not to cry all over again. She later sent a condolence card that read: "It's been a hard year on us bunny lovers! Brenda." She had lost her beloved bunny, Logan, the week before. He'd had mouth problems and skin problems and Brenda had tended to him and taken him to numerous vets for over two weeks before finally deciding to end his misery.

The other thing Brenda pointed out to reduce my depression was that Magic lived five and a half years in our care, and had had free run of a bedroom most of the time. Once I figured out a towel on the floor could bridge the gap called the wooden floor separating the bedrooms from the living room, Magic had occasional access to the main room of our house. Once I figured out he didn't like any fresh vegetation and in fact preferred chocolate PopTarts, I made those a daily treat. After a couple of years, I knew that if he sat down next to his water bowl at night, I could pet him; if he walked away, I could not. Like every other creature that had come into my life, I had done my best to figure out what made Magic tick and how to spoil him.

Mark said Magic was a great name for the white bunny with the black rim around his eye, because he touched us in magical ways. He had personality. There were things he liked and things he didn't like, and he figured out ways to tells us. He was part of our everyday for a long time. As with Bumpkin, I'm not sure we still even understand why he touched us so.

As with every other creature that had come into our lives, I had fallen for Magic and my heart had been broken in the end. This one hurt especially because it was my fault. Only by focusing on the good that had come—the magic that Magic brought—could I move on.

During times like that I wonder whether the heartache of losing a fuzzy or feathery pal is worth the months or years we have with the fuzzy or feathery. Every critter that Mark always wanted, and the ones like Magic that he hadn't known he always wanted, brought us years of unconditional love. Well, except maybe Coco. And with the passing of each and every one—except maybe Coco—came tears and sadness that lasted days, weeks, sometimes months. But each and every time, as the pain subsides and the good memories beat out the bad—except for maybe Coco—the answer to whether it is worth it to love these critters is always yes. Even for Coco.

Tip #47: Your spouse's definition of a "full house" may be different than yours.

CHAPTER 9

Just When I Thought I had Everything

In 2009, Pinky the guinea pig died after a brief illness. We were in Montana at the time and Melissa said she knew something was wrong when Pinky started breathing in raspy gasps. Luckily, Conrad was around to help Melissa remove the dead critter and bury him in the backyard. And luckily, it was summer, so Pinky stayed buried.

Lincoln carried on alone, wheeking at me every time I went by his cage, until late summer 2010, when I walked by to let the dogs out and heard no "wheek" from the cage. When I checked on Lincoln and saw he was still alive, I attributed his lack of calling to the fact that I was so trained to feed him every time I walked by, he had no need to call any more. Still, it bothered me. I missed his call. But since he was eating like a pig, I didn't think much more about it.

About four months later, in January, though, Lincoln stopped eating the fresh grapes he used to inhale, and began merely nibbling on celery pieces. Some days, he left the fresh dandelion greens to rot on the bottom of the cage, some days he only nibbled on a fresh strawberry. Since he also wasn't eating much dry food, I added hot water to his Mardi Gras guinea pig food. Such a trick had worked well for my elderly ferrets, but Lincoln didn't care for the mush at all.

On January 24, after I let the dogs out, I stopped by to check on Lincoln. For reasons I can't explain, I found myself reaching out to him, and this time, when I touched him on the head, he did not move away. I stroked his head, told him he'd been a good pig, and hoped I'd done well by him. The next morning, I found him lying on his side. It appeared as if he'd been about to tug at a piece of timothy from the side of his cage and simply laid down to rest. For a critter that was only supposed to live up to eight years, the fact that Lincoln lived to the ripe old age of 12 was pretty amazing. Mark said we definitely got our money's worth when we got Lincoln.

For a week afterward, Mark and Elizabeth both found themselves carrying fresh strawberry bits from the kitchen and around the corner to Lincoln's cage, only to turn around with a sad face because Lincoln was no longer there.

Now, you remember what happened to Sox when Mark tried to bury him in the winter? Well, we agreed that the skulls of our pets wouldn't rise from the ground again, so, it being January when Lincoln died, we tucked him in a red shoebox and put the box in the chest freezer in the garage. Fast forward a week later to Elizabeth's 21st birthday party when Mark asked me to run out to see if there was any French vanilla ice cream in the freezer. I really wasn't thinking about dead animals when I lifted the lid to look for ice cream, but, there on top of everything, in the center of the freezer was the box with Lincoln inside. I really didn't want to disturb the box, and really, really didn't want to move it at all, so I carefully moved a roast out of the way, only to notice the red shoebox move a little toward the left side of the freezer. I moved a pie box out of the way and the red shoebox moved again. I moved a chicken, saw that the ice cream beneath it was butter pecan, put the chicken back, and slammed the lid shut. I went back inside and announced sorry, we had no French vanilla ice cream.

Come the spring 2011, we gave Lincoln a proper burial. And I found some French vanilla in the bottom of the freezer.

Tip #48: Even fish can be stressful.

In preparation for his retirement in the spring of 2012, Mark decided to take the summer of 2011 off to see what it would be like. That means he did not drive the hour-long jaunt up to Alma College to try to keep college summer interns busy and he did not work on any research projects and he did not, in fact, do much of anything. For a while.

I've mentioned before that I knew it was a matter of time before something new would come into my life, but I was still surprised when two square, "swooshing" boxes arrived containing a total of seven discus fish. Mark claimed that the brightly colored, discus-shaped fish would add beauty to our 90 gallon aquarium. Now, I don't really "do fish." I'd rather swim with them than watch them in an aquarium, but when I looked at the aquarium's current residents, four-inch-long silver tetras with the black vertical lines and the few neon and other smaller tetras, I thought maybe Mark had a point. The aquarium was pretty boring. I also recalled that Mark's elephant nose fish had died a few years back and he'd been rather devastated, so if a few discus fish made him happy, what did I care?

So I admitted that our tank was boring, and admitted, too, that I didn't know much about discus fish. I did, however, recall seeing some rather large discus fish in aquariums somewhere, so I suspected discus fish could get big. I also know that boys sometimes fight with other boys. But while I was worried about lots of large fish fighting it out in one aquarium, Mark happily took each fish from their watery container, and dumped them into a plastic Ziploc® bag suspended in the fish tank to give them time to adjust to the new water temperature. He also spoke to them occasionally, saying things like, "Hold on guys, you'll be free and in your new home in a little while." An hour later, all seven fish were swimming about the tank, most of them probably wondering what the heck had happened to them over the course of the last few days.

It turns out the eight-year-old silver tetras didn't like the new invaders and ganged up on them. This involved pushing and shoving, which stressed Mark out. The discus fish also had to develop their own pecking order amongst themselves, which involved a lot of pushing and shoving in what seemed, to me anyway, to be a very small aquarium. This also stressed Mark out. Two discus fish took to hiding behind plants most of the time. One developed a wound on its back. This really stressed Mark out.

Not surprisingly, all the pushing and shoving and wounds and potential for more wounds put Mark over the edge. One day he borrowed my Honda Element (which always makes me suspicious), and returned a few hours later with a new aquarium. And not just any aquarium. It was oddly shaped, made completely of clear plastic and came with a nice base that fit the shape of the aquarium. I estimated the aquarium would hold about 75 gallons of water.

By this time in our marriage, our ferret-chewed La-Z-Boy chair had been provided a new home, which freed up some space in our living room and allowed the new tank to go in the corner of the room next to the fireplace. As Mark set up the new tank, he stopped by the old aquarium now and then and said, "Hey guys, some of you are going to get a new home!"

Mark spent the next full day running water through the new water osmosis machine he'd also purchased for these "very special fish," as he called them. What amused me was that he set up the osmosis machine in the basement, which meant he had to run up and down the stairs with full buckets of water. I was pleased to see Mark was willing to go to such an extent for his fish.

Two days later, after the water was just so and we had new, colorful plants and everything looked pretty in the new tank, Mark went about the business of trying to net the bad tetras. This is an under-rated sport if you ask me. I stood back and watched for about five full minutes, giggling heartily as Mark chased the fast, skinny fish around the tank. Finally, he turned to me and said, "Wouldn't it be nice of you to help?"

"But watching you is so much more amusing," I said before sighing and grabbing a second net.

With two people attacking the bad tetras, it was much easier. Several minutes later, having dripped all sorts of water on the carpet, we stood back and eyeballed the two most aggressive—a.k.a. bad—discus fish. We knew one was blue and one was orange, but since all the fish were blue or orange, we stood there—nets dripping on the floor—trying to determine which ones were the bad ones.

Five minutes later, we'd nabbed what we hoped were the bad ones and, after wiping up the floor and washing our arms and hands, we sat back and watched the new tank. All seemed right with the "bad" fish. Then we watched the old tank. One discus fish was poking and prodding the other ones.

"It's possible they're just re-establishing the pecking order," I said.

And so we decided to just keep an eye on them.

All was well in the fish tanks until about a week later, when one of the blue discus fish died. So, of course, Mark became immediately paranoid about the others getting sick and went into action checking the hardness, the alkalinity, the temperature and pretty much everything about the water except the taste (thank goodness). He reverse-osmosized more water to replace some water he deemed less than perfect, all the while talking to the fish: "Hey little dudes, I'm trying to make this all right for you." Later, after improving the water to his satisfaction, he said, "There, guys. You should be all happy now."

"Do they talk back, and say, `Hey there, big guy, thanks for lookin' out for us?'" I asked.

Mark stuck his tongue out at me and went off for more good water for the Bad Fish tank. Of course, he didn't like it that I called it the Bad Fish tank, but let's get a little fish spine in us, shall we?

All was well again in the world of discus fish until about two weeks later, when Mark discovered eggs stuck to the long, skinny tube-like heater in the big aquarium. And so I wondered: *Do we need to turn the heater off? What are the odds these fish eggs will hatch? With all those adult fish in there, won't the eggs or babies get eaten?*

Perhaps wondering at least one of these same things, Mark turned off the heater and then fretted about whether to turn the air pump off—thinking that the babies would get sucked up into the pump if, in fact, the eggs hatched. He retested the water and told the fish not to eat the eggs. He also counted the money he would make if he could sell discus babies to the pet stores. Me? I was thinking about how the hedgehog market crashed after Mark's great expectations for them and told him not to count his fish before they hatched.

Unfortunately, the eggs did get eaten, and after the loving couple—two beautiful blue discus—laid and ate another set of eggs, Mark got online and read that we needed to separate the parents from the rest of the fish. He, of course, was thinking about a third aquarium. I suggested we first try bringing the Bad Guys back to the bigger tank and move Mom and Dad Discus to the new, smaller tank and see how that goes. If that didn't work, I would concede to a third aquarium.

And so another evening was spent netting fish and moving them to a different aquarium, watching them re-establish a pecking order, testing the water, adding more good water and removing old water. When I closed my eyes that night, I could see colorful smears swimming left and right under my tired eyelids.

The next day, Mark read online somewhere that mating male and female discus fish prefer to have an aquarium free of plants, so he removed all the plants from the new aquarium. Three more sets of eggs were laid and eaten and I finally suggested that perhaps our fish were different—perhaps they were the weird discus that liked plants to hide in and which, gee, would also provide hiding places for their babies. A week after a couple of plants were added to the new aquarium, Mom and Dad gave birth to a bunch of little disci. The babies looked like little sperm and spent the first part of their lives nibbling on the mucus on the sides of their parents. Days later, the parents ate the babies anyway.

Tip #49: Hamster is German for hoarder. Not all hoarders are the same.

It wasn't enough for Mark's pre-retirement summer to just bring a bunch of stressful, albeit colorful, fish into my house, Mark also fell for a hamster. Then another and—.

It began without discussion or warning: I simply came home from work one day and saw a two-level hamster cage on my kitchen counter. It was blue and green and happened to match one of my kitchen towels, which, of course, matched nothing else in my kitchen. Inside the cage was a pale orange, super fuzzy, really cute hamster that had hair going in every direction possible. He was about twice the size of Hammy, our very first hamster. I asked Mark about our new visitor and he merely said, "His name is Little Buddha because he looks like a little Buddha when he sits on his haunches and munches on something."

Sure enough, when I peeked inside at the orange fuzzy, he was eating a Wheat Thin and he did look like a Little Buddha. To introduce myself to our new pet, I took a Spanish peanut from a container on the counter and held it out between the metal bars on the bottom of the cage. Little Buddha came over, and, without sniffing, took the peanut out of my fingers so quickly I didn't know what hit me. When I pulled my hand back, I felt a bolt of pain in my finger and saw two small holes with tiny drops of blood on them.

"Uh, wasn't the real Buddha big on meditation and calmness?" I asked Mark.

"Yes."

"Well, I find a wee bit of a contradiction in the fact that Little Buddha bites the hand that feeds him."

Mark sighed as he walked over and showed me how to take a food item and hold it at the tip of my fingers so that

Little Buddha couldn't bite. He offered Buddha a Wheat Thin, held it on the far edge and Buddha took it gently from Mark's hand. I encouraged Mark to try to give Buddha a Spanish peanut. As I predicted, Buddha took it fast as a snapping turtle and Mark pulled back his hand to see two snake-bite-like marks on his fingers.

Because Little Buddha bit the careless feeder, Mark said he wasn't exactly the hamster he was looking for, so he set out to buy another hamster. At the time he set out to buy his second hamster, the hamster market was at a low and he found very few to choose from. After searching no fewer than five Lansing area pet stores, he stumbled upon this reddish-brown, super fuzzy, rather cute hamster that had one eye larger than the other and had been overlooked dozens of times in no less than two different pet stores. She was in a very small cage, so Mark credits himself for rescuing her.

The hamster he named Nibs was at once the best hamster in the world, the one Mark had always wanted, the most interactive, cutest fuzzy thing in the world. Nibs came up to the side of the cage to see Mark in the morning and took pumpkin seeds and sunflower seeds and various treats from Mark in the gentlest of fashion. In fact, as with Buddha, just about every time we walked through the kitchen— where everyone should keep their hamsters, by the way— Nibs would come out from her round ball of bedding and tissues and come over to see what we had to offer. And unlike Little Buddha, Nibs could be petted. Nibs' cage was different than Buddha's in that it had a tube in the middle to climb to a second level that covered most of the cage. Within days, Nibs had gnawed her way through part of the second level so as to better plant herself against the side of the cage to receive treats.

Now, the fact that Mark was in love with Nibs isn't all

that surprising, but the fact that he got a third hamster remains quite confusing to me. A couple of weeks after the arrival of Nibs, I came home from work to find a third cage on my kitchen counter. Inside was this black and white, short-haired panda hamster. She looked nothing like the other two and was as smooth as the other two were fuzzy. For the black and white hamster, Mark purchased a third cage with a tiny plastic compartment at the top, which was where the hamster slept at night surrounded by bedding and tiny bits of tissues.

The black and white hamster went nameless for about a week. Then, less than a week after she came into our home, I awoke one morning to comment on how chubby she'd gotten in the few days she'd been with us. When she appeared larger the next day, Mark and I both went "Uh oh" at the same time. On day seven, the hamster we named Mom had eight naked, blind, helpless babies that were about a half inch long.

Immediately, paranoia set in because Mark and I both knew that stressed mom hamsters sometimes eat their babies. She could also crush them, and it was possible they might wander down from their nest at the top of their cage and fall down the tube and get stuck. And if you can imagine all the other bad things that could happen to a baby hamster, well, we imagined it first. Every night we discussed whether to remove Mom and the babies from the little container at the top of Mom's cage, whether to clean out the bedding, or whether to pile the bedding up around the lip of the tube so no babies would fall down the tube.

A few weeks went by and the first baby started walking, so we moved the top container inside a larger container. Then we worried that wasn't good, because if the babies got out, well, would Mom go find them or would they freeze to death alone? So we took piles of hamster bedding and made barriers so that Mom could come and go from the new cage and the babies could not. We checked on them at all times of the day and many times before we went to bed, too, because we were determined not to lose any of the babies, even if there were eight of them.

At some point, it occurred to me that the babies would soon be big and hairy and need new homes. So, when the hamster babies were only a few weeks old, I started pitching them at work and to our friends. When my photos didn't result in any sales and the babies kept growing, I found myself agreeing to help my co-workers and answer their questions only if they agreed to take a baby hamster. All of them walked away, hamsterless.

We also told the pet store where we'd purchased Mom about our influx of babies, and their response was that another person who'd gotten a hamster recently also ended up with eight babies. They added that considering we'd only paid for one, we got quite a great deal!

The babies kept growing and their crawling turned into walking. One day, even when their eyes were still not open, we took some of the babies and put them on the table to take photos. We also introduced them to tomato bits. I must say it was odd watching a blind hamster baby nibbling on a tomato bit.

When their eyes finally did open, I swear they all blinked at us in unison as if sending some bizarre signal that they had landed right where they'd intended to land. It was while blinking back at them one night and hearing Mark chattering behind me about the various types of cages he was ordering that I knew: The hamsters were here to stay.

At about four weeks, we got online to figure out how to separate boys from girls, which is really quite simple unless you screw it up, in which case, you'll have more babies. What you do is lift up one hamster and compare the underside of one to the other like you do mice. If the two holes on one are spaced like the other, you have two hamsters of the same sex. If their holes are spaced differently, you have a boy and a girl. And if you wait long enough that the boys have genitalia that make their gender easy to identify, well, it might already be too late.

We'd also read online that not only do we have to separate boys from girls, we should be prepared to separate boys from boys when they mature and decide they don't like each other anymore. So, we separated boys from girls, discovered a few unsociable girls, and a boy that didn't like anybody and ended up with eight hamster cages in all. The cage holding three boys consists of three levels. The one for two girls has two levels. Two are Habitrail OVO cages, which are space-age looking round units with attachments, allowing one of our hamsters—a late addition named Flip—to make a full square running up and down tubes in her cage. Yes, even with all the hamsters we already had, there was room for one more, said Mark.

With so many hamster cages, not only was our kitchen counter full, our front entryway—which once housed the guinea pigs—was also full.

Having so many hamsters was not a task to be taken lightly. Their cages required daily attention. For example, two of the black and white hamsters slept in the top, removable container of their cage, which, for some strange reason, is the same place they used as a bathroom. Yuck. That container was emptied almost every day. On the other hand, Flip had a room that she used for her bathroom, which was separate from the room she used to sleep in and also the room she recreated in, so her cage only needed to be cleaned once a week.

All the hamsters had wheels to run on because Mark read that a hamster can run eight miles on their wheels, "and imagine how horrible it would be to be without one." Some hamsters urinated while running on their wheels, which meant their wheels needed to be cleaned fairly often. It also meant that they were too lazy to get off their wheel to relieve themselves, which makes no sense at all.

Nibs was one of the neater hamsters, separating her pooping area from her sleeping area and from her stash pile. She took the task of hoarding to a new level, separating her dry goods—like Wheat Thins and Cheerios—from perishables—like bits of grapes and tomatoes. She also continued to interact with us daily. When Mark's nephew, Terry, visited and wondered what Nibs was, we realized that Nibs truly was an odd looking little hamster. And, said Mark, a special one. Nibs would remain his favorite.

Summer turned into fall and I noticed that Nibs showed signs of slowing down. When we let her run around in an enclosure on the floor while we cleaned out her cage, we noticed her tail and rear end was wet, as if she'd sat down in a pool of water. Thing is, there was no standing water in her cage. Mark got online and learned that Nibs likely had wet tail, an incurable intestinal disease common in large hamsters. In addition to the wet tail, the hamster slows down, stops eating, and eventually dies. Within a week after learning about wet tail, and in spite of Mark getting some antibiotic for Nibs to fight the disease, Nibs was gone.

Tip #50: Big guys can get all mushy about small critters.

Mark was devastated by Nibs' death. He cried as he held her during her final hours. He cried when he buried her and said, "You were the best, Nibs and I hope you have fun in heaven." He talked about her for days (really, weeks) afterwards, telling me all of her good qualities and what made her so special. He talked about the way she came to the cage in the morning to see what treats he had to offer, how she liked being petted, how she once got a hold of his t-shirt and bit and pulled and screamed a crazy scream, we think, because she wanted it for her own. I never knew a big fella could be so crushed by the loss of a fuzzy creature that weighed mere ounces.

Within weeks, the Mom of all the hamsters was the next victim of wet tail. She, too, lasted about a week before going off to Hamster Heaven.

It wasn't until the summer of 2012—about six months after Mom died—that we lost our next hamster: Little Buddha. He was the first of the fuzzy hamsters, the one that greeted me in the morning and the one I tucked in at night during his last few months when biting no longer seemed the thing to do. In fact, I knew Little Buddha was in trouble when I could actually pet him. He developed a golf ball-size tumor in May (which popped like the most disgusting of pimples) and he died just about the time the first tumor seemed to be healing over. Turns out, there was another, bigger tumor underneath. Mark, fully retired in 2012, held Little Buddha during his final hours.

The day Little Buddha died, my dad was in the hospital because his kidneys had failed in response to his second round of chemotherapy. Shortly after Little Buddha was buried (the ceremony of which included "God bless Little Buddha"), I spent five minutes to cry for the fuzzy creature that had greeted me every morning for over a year and made me laugh. Then I cried for the first of many, many times for my father—the man that is the gentlest man I have ever known and whose sense of humor remained in place even when the chips were down. And when he was out of chips altogether.

I drove the hour long drive to Grand Rapids to visit my father many times during the spring and summer of 2012. On most visits with my dad, Mark claimed I blabbed on mercilessly about the status of the critters in my house, the critters in my backyard, and even the little fox squirrel that I saw outside my office in downtown Lansing who came right up to me to lap water out of the Styrofoam cup I brought out for him one 90 degree day. I think my dad was okay with my blathering, because he'd taken in stray cats over the years, and shot one deer ever in his life, after which "hunting" became "spending quality time with my gun in the woods." He liked all critters, and even tolerated the female groundhog in his backyard that had dug numerous holes under his shed. In the spring of 2012, that female groundhog had six babies, so on one of my last visits to my Dad's I brought a bag of apples and had a contest with my niece and nephew to see who could roll the apples closest to the shed without the apple falling into the groundhogs' hole. On the last day I was able to chat with my father, I dedicated my book to him. In response he said, "Thanks, that's very sweet of you." Then, after pausing for a moment he added, "But do me a favor. Don't bring any more apples. We really don't want to encourage seven groundhogs to stay in the yard."

To which I said, "Gosh, can we have one?"

EPILOGUE

So far, my marriage has outlasted frogs, iguanas, hedgehogs, ferrets, a rabbit, a duck, two dogs, a cat, two guinea pigs, and countless mice, gerbils and hamsters. I tell my friends that I always have something to look forward to—I just don't know exactly what it will be. Consider late summer 2012 when I found myself waiting around the Delta Cargo section of Detroit Metropolitan Airport for the arrival of a mynah bird Mark had ordered from Florida. A few weeks later, we "accidentally" wound up with another mynah bird, but more on that later.

My ongoing problem, of course, is that every critter that enters our house has surprised me—the things it does, the food it likes, the things that comfort or scare it. I remain amazed at how unique each critter is and how quickly they became part of my world. I am also perpetually amazed at the endless number of them that Mark still wants and, because of that, I made a "Honey Don't List" that includes "Going to a pet store unsupervised."

Among our second batch of ferrets, Hoppie was the first to leave us after developing a tumor on his stomach. I found him lethargic and moaning one day in 2010, so we took him to a vet for a formal diagnosis and to end his suffering. The fact that it cost $110 to end Hoppie's suffering was a bit disturbing. The fact that the vet was still "sorry for our loss" left me speechless. I wanted to tell him that I was sorry our loss cost so much.

The other three ferrets—Smiggles, Chip and Peanut—all began losing the fur on their tails and backs in early 2010. This happened to our first batch of ferrets when they were six or so and we'd associated such hair loss before to kidney failure. But since Smiggles and company were only four when they developed the problem, I was wondering if something else was up. So, I bought vitamins and different food, added water to other food in the house, and finally, I stumbled upon the idea adding warm water to a plate of kitten food and squeezing the food bits. Smiggles lapped up the water instantly and loved the soft food. Then Chip noticed, then Peanut, and suddenly all three of them looked for the soggy mixture every night. And, magically, the fur grew back on their back and tails. Peanut lived another six months, Smiggles six months after that.

As of March 2013, Chip was the last remaining ferret, slowly winding down. Play time lasted about five minutes, upon which time she'd nibble on a treat I left for her and then find a place to make a nest in our pile of laundry or in some sweatshirts and towels I left in a spare bedroom just for her. It took me almost seven years to figure out her favorite snack: Friskies Party Mix Beachside Crunch, particularly the Meow Luau flavor. (Handily, Dusty and Purrkins love those as well). I also discovered two ways of mobilizing an elderly ferret: putting her in a shoebox with a string tied to it and dragging the box across the floor with her little head sticking out a hole I cut in the front of the box; and folding her up in Dusty's large bed cushion and carrying her inches above the floor like a hovercraft. Chip passed away right before Easter snuggled up in one of my old sweatshirts.

Purrkins is still part of the fabric of our daily life and has just reached middle age . . . unless cats really do have nine lives, in which case he's just a kitten still. He is amazing at getting what he wants—morning rub-downs, nibbles of Dusty's soft dog food, tidbits of human food, naps whenever and wherever he wants. I mean, I tell Mark I want lobster for dinner and I get it once in 18 years. Purrkins gets salmon pâté on a regular basis. I just don't get it.

I need to confess here that I felt left out about not having my own hamster, so I got myself one who now resides in our small bathroom. She's mostly blonde in color, and I'm afraid she's the slowest one we've ever had—she doesn't know how to shred little pieces of toilet paper and tissues to make her nest (so I shred pieces for her), and she seems to have an aversion to tubes, which means she uses only the bottom floor of her two-story cage. Like a stereotypical blonde, though, the hamster I named Daisy makes up for her lack of brains by being very, very cute.

Mark and I ended up moving the other hamsters off the kitchen counter and into a room we called The Hamster Room. It happened after one black and white panda hamster died because we'd left a latch open after cleaning out all the cages and the hamster got out of her cage and fell onto the floor. In their own room on low storage containers, any hamster escapees—and we've had several—can't fall very far and are contained in the bedroom. Sadly, though, even in the protection of their own room, our hamsters seem to average a lifespan of only about 12 months. To make the best of those few months, our hamsters get nuts, tomato slices, sunflower seeds, and carrots to supplement their usual hamster food. In addition, most nights, we have up to five hamster balls rolling around our living room floor.

Unlike our short-lived hamsters, Dusty turned 14 in July 2012, which is like 98 in people years according to an old myth. The cool thing is that, unlike old people, old dogs don't sit around talking about the surgery that Bob the Beagle had, or how Charles the Spaniel wasn't looking so good when we were on a walk lately, and, gee, I wonder what's up with him? Dogs live for the moment. They're not too proud to be lifted onto the bed when they are no longer spritely enough to do so on their own, and they adapt quite well to a new bolster purchased to ease their way off a bed. They're quite happy to just walk along a beach rather than run in and out of the cool water, and when we stopped going on pups vacations in 2010, they didn't whine about it . . . unlike Mark, who whined because he "no longer gets to sleep on the lumpy, hard, cold ground, wake up stiff as a board having to pee badly." Cheerful fella, isn't he?

As the dogs got older, our daily walk changed as well, because sometimes Dusty wanted to go on a walk, sometimes he didn't. If he wanted to walk with Dipper and me, we'd head down the street, and at some designated point known only to Dusty, he'd stiffen his legs and barrel his chest, turn around and head towards home. Talking him out of it was like talking to a V8 engine, so Dipper and I simply followed. Once we got back, I dropped Dusty off, and Dipper and I went off on a second, longer walk.

Dipper was not only my walking pal, she was my traveling buddy. She'd go anywhere with me in the car, and became a bit of a celebrity at the local McDonald's because we went through the drive-thru every weekend morning to get a sausage patty and a sausage biscuit for the dogs' breakfast. It was a habit—and a good one, I'm sure—that we'd developed in 2010 after Dipper's last bad teeth were pulled. To her diet of sausage, canned ravioli and Beneful soft food, we also added a product from the freezer section of the pet store called Nature's Variety Instinct Raw Frozen Diet. These are pricey frozen medallions made of 95% meat, organs and bones and 5% veggies. You put them in the fridge overnight and they're soft enough to snarf. The dogs loved them.

While Dipper lacked teeth, Dusty's were mostly in good shape, so we continued giving him tiny bits of baby carrots every night between 7:30 and 8:00. I'm not sure how we got into that, but if I happen to forget, he reminds me by whining at me until I get up and start chopping.

We were not, however, prepared for Dusty becoming ultra sensitive to noise, which was followed by becoming completely deaf. His deafness proved the old adage that it's hard to teach an old dog new tricks—Dusty did not take to my Parkinson's-like hand signals quickly and I kept on talking to him in spite of him not hearing a single word. In fact, early on, getting Dusty outside required Mark to wave him to the door while I poked gently from behind. Dusty's deafness also made it such that he no longer played with—or guarded us with—his squeaky toys. That made me sad. In fact, at times the only bit of humor I could find in having two old dogs was telling people that while Dusty was deaf and Dipper had no teeth, between the two of them, they made for a really great watch dog.

Over the summer of 2012, we also noticed more changes in Little Dipper. By early summer, she didn't jump up and down when I got the leash out for a walk and she seemed just as content getting her belly rubbed on the couch, kind of like Mark. The spring in her step was replaced by a type of waddle, which I attributed to arthritis in her front left shoulder and her back right leg. Dusty, too, was slowing down, and his back legs gave out on him sometimes as he walked up and down a step.

Because my father was in and out of the hospital during June and July 2012, I spent a lot of time in Grand Rapids and barely noticed that coinciding with my dad's decline was Dipper's continued decline in energy. When Dipper was poky slow on a walk around our lake in late July, I attributed it to the heat. On shorter walks around the neighborhood, I attributed Dipper's slowness to the fact that it was hot AND we hadn't gotten her trimmed in a while. As my dad declined, there were a few nights Dipper didn't get a walk at all, and she seemed all too happy to head back to the couch with Mark. I just figured she was getting old.

My father passed away August 11 and we held his military funeral four days later. Afterwards, back at home, I sought sanctity in a nice long walk with Dipper, only to discover she wasn't up for walking any further than a half dozen houses. I thought perhaps her toenails were bothering her in addition to being wooly, arthritic and hot, so set up an appointment to get her groomed.

Several more evenings passed. On the evening of August 26, Little Dipper, Dusty and I were walking like three old snails, and after about 200 yards, Dusty decided it was time to turn around. The air was warm, perhaps 75 degrees, and when we returned, Dipper did not look up at me to go for a longer walk. I unhooked both dogs' leashes and went about playing with Chip. Around 8:00 or so I let Dipper outside and noticed she was walking as if her legs were weighted down. She'd acted like an old lady many times before—

when we'd made her go outside when she didn't want to—but this seemed different somehow. As I watched her sluggishly wander around the yard, then stand and stare as if unseeing, I knew something wasn't quite right. Mark thought her tummy seemed rounder than usual, so perhaps I just overfed her. The very idea made me feel horrible.

Little Dipper spent the next couple of hours lying on the couch, but not upside down getting her tummy rubbed as in the past. She'd had upset stomach issues before and had been stand-offish before, so we didn't think too much of that, either. Come 10:00, though, she seemed so sluggish that I found myself carrying her outside to do her business. I watched her walk so very slowly on her way up the steps, and it was the way she looked at me—almost sad, far away, maybe? —that got me to worrying.

Because she was acting funny, Mark and I debated whether to let Dipper sleep with us in our bed. Her stomach seemed bloated and I said something about not being crazy about her getting sick in bed. But Mark said otherwise. And I'm so glad he did.

About an hour after we went to sleep we heard a funny noise—a whine, a moan. Mark turned on the light and we saw Dipper pawing at the air. Mark lifted her off the bed and supported her on the floor as she whined a little and barfed up her dinner. Still hoping she was just sick, Mark tried letting go of her, only to see she had no strength on her left side.

We took Little Dipper to the MSU Small Animal Clinic. Within an hour, the kindly vet and her sweet technician told us as gingerly as possible that Little Dipper had had a stroke and had no function of any kind on the left side of her body. They took us to a small room with softly cushioned seats and plenty of boxes of Kleenex and brought Dipper in on a towel.

When Dipper saw us her tail wagged back and forth, back and forth, like it never had before. Her tongue was hanging out of her toothless mouth and she pawed at my face with her right front paw while her left one was motionless. The vet said they'd give us a few minutes to be alone with her and I said, "No, please, I don't want to see her suffer a moment longer." The vet had come prepared and knelt down on the floor next to Mark, while I sat on the couch with Dipper's head where I could pet her. Mark told her what a good dog she was, and said so many other nice things I did not hear, because I was speaking, too. I nodded through tears to the vet, who administered the first injection. In seconds, Dipper went limp. The vet's eyes were filled with tears as she said, "Dipper knew she was loved." Then the vet administered the final injection and Little Dipper breathed her last with the four of us crying at her side.

During the brief eternity that followed, Mark and I sat in the tiny room wiping our eyes and wondering out loud if we'd done okay by Dipper, if there had been anything else we could have or should have done at this moment. We agreed we had done okay by her, and that it was a miracle she had any fur left on her tummy given all the tummy rubs Mark had given her.

When it seemed we had nothing more to say, we stepped out into the lobby and met the vet and vet tech coming down the hall with a plain brown box. The box felt heavy in my arms and the very weight of my pal brought more tears to my eyes. The vet told us she was sorry for our loss and waved at the clerk at the door to indicate that they'd send the bill later. We thanked her and drove home with our little pal at 1:30 a.m. We left the box in the bathroom overnight.

I had a meeting at work the next morning, so I numbly went about the business of being a good state worker, pretending to be cheerful and professional. I returned home to find Mark digging a grave in the concrete-hard dirt. I grabbed the pick and he the shovel and we finished up together. Back inside, we took Dipper's box and put it on the floor, the idea being to give Purrkins and Dusty a chance to say good-bye. Purrkins ran off and wasn't seen again until later in the day. Dusty strolled over slowly, sniffing as he walked warily up to the box, as if building up the nerve. When at last he reached the box, he leaned over and gently grabbed Dipper by the ear and pulled, as if trying to get her up. It was the saddest thing I've ever seen.

We carried Dipper outside and buried her. "God bless the little dog that could get us to do anything with a simple blink of her dark brown eyes. May she run happily across the heavens."

With winter just around the corner and no empty space in our chest freezer, Conrad dug a grave for Dusty next to Dipper's "just in case." The ¼-inch piece of plywood covering Dusty's grave was visible from the bay window and seeing it, the falling leaves and Dusty's wobbly back legs gave me a strong sense of passing time.

From chapter 4 of this book on, Dusty was the one constant—the angel pup that was kind to one critter after another—and I suddenly needed to get his story told while he was around. It wasn't like he'd go with me to a book signing or anything but I went with the notion anyway.

As I wrote, I tried not to think about Dusty's eventual demise or the recent losses. Instead, I tried to focus on how much joy Mark had unwittingly brought into my life over the years and how I had fallen for each and every critter that made our house a home.

See, every fuzzy and feathery critter that enters our lives has a story. And I believe it is our job as humans to make their stories as good as possible. For me, that's clearly a work in progress, as you'll see in the following brief stories as told by the critters themselves.

Mama Gerbil's Story:

I once thought plankton were on the bottom of the food chain, but in colleges and places that raise nasty, gnarly snakes, it's us gerbils and mice. Can you imagine being born for the sole purpose of feeding another creature kept for man's amusement?

So, imagine how much we love the man that rescued us—me and my Man Gerbil, that is. Oh, it's a bummer we had to get separated after the babies, but we had a good life all in all. Well, except that day behind the refrigerator—that was scary. And the dust—you can't imagine the dust behind that fridge! But once I got off the refrigerator coils and onto the floor, I was rescued, brushed off and put into a new cage. From then on, we got lots of box-board to chew, plenty to eat and the opportunity to use our exercise wheel whenever we felt like it, which, I must say, is more often than the humans used their elliptical machine.

Chunky's Story:

I don't really like speaking poorly of critters, but, well, Coco wasn't my favorite. She was awfully bite-y and about the best thing about her was when she snuggled up with me to keep warm at night. Sometimes I dreamed about other play pals, but knew Mom and Dad were committed to keeping critters even if they weren't the most ideal.

Mom and Dad knew that ferrets like to have other ferret pals to play with, and it wasn't too long after Coco died before Rocky came along. He was a bit like Coco, the way he went after plants, the way he ran away the exact moment Mom or Dad came after us to put us away. But he was a good ferret all and all, especially when he was older and a little less devilish.

I was real happy when Sox came along—he was gentle like me and had this weird fascination with Beanie Babies. I always thought that if by some bizarre piece of luck a female ferret showed up, he'd ignore her, preferring the company of the Beanies over hers.

Big Wuzzy came from Maryland and was part English, which means he was supposed to be real big and have a hankering for tea and scones or something. Dad had hoped for a bread-loaf size ferret, but Big Wuzzy was more like a baguette, Dad said. But Dad loved him nonetheless. Big Wuzzy loved to play and after tackling any human and ferret in sight, he'd head right to the cupboard and push open the drawer with kitchen towels in it, because he'd trained Mom to give him treats there. What was funny was that while Big Wuzzy burned up lots of his energy to get treats, all I had to do is look pathetic. It worked every time. I got bits of Dad's bananas, bits of bagels (with lots of butter, please), raisins and ferret treats.

So it was a good life all in all, with our own snuggy cage, lots of buddies to play with, lots of treats, a little bit of human contact. I even got to check out the furnace ducts one day, which, you might imagine, left me with a coating of dust on my fur. The only bummer was that there were so many animals in the house, there was no time for Mom and Dad to let me be a true advocate for safe cages for ferrets—you know, cages with so many hammocks and soft things that the longest fall is four inches onto soft bedding. There are lots of bad ferret cages still out there, even at pet stores.

The lady wrote a book about us called Good-night, Big Wuzzy. It's a children's photo book. You should get it because I'm in it and Mom says I'm one of the nicest ferrets in the world.

Purrkins' Story:

About the only thing my mom told me when she dropped me off under this deck was that I needed to look pitiful and cute in order to be taken in-side. And she was right! This lady saw me and I mewed softly and she brought out some food and milk. She moved real slowly and talked softly, but then she pushed the food toward me and reached for me, so I ran off to the kayak and spent another night alone.

Two more nights went by just like that and the next evening I was pushed from behind into this plastic box-like cage. It had shiny metal bars on it and I played with those as I went inside a bedroom. There, a big scary guy said something about me dying if I bit him. To show him how nice I was, as soon as he touched me, I purred. He stroked my head and I purred and purred and turned into fuzzy mush. I won the big guy over just like that.

I was back in the cage the next morning and in a car to this place with fuzzy creatures they say were like me. This scary lady that smelled like medicine looked me over and poked me with the needle to kill of the nasty lice and fleas I had picked up outside.

Once I got myself inside the peoples' house, I continued finding ways to get what I wanted. The lady was pretty easy to train. All I have to do is run in front of her and fall over and she'll pet me. After she's dressed in the morning, I walk in front of her to lead her to my empty plate, looking all pitiful and skinny even though I'm not anymore. She fills up my bowl and gives me kitty treats and bits of Dusty's dog food, which I like sometimes and sometimes not. She also makes sure I always have fresh water even though the toilet is still my favorite watering hole. When I want the man to pet me, I jump on whatever chair is nearby and he usually gives me a good rub down.

I spend my day "hunting" birds that land on the tiny feeder stuck to the bay window, tackling one of a dozen or so fake fuzzy mice lying around the house, and taking naps. At night, the lady hides behind chairs and rolls balls and fake mice down the hall for me to chase. When the man and lady go off to bed, I sit on the man's new retirement chair by the new bay window, and dream of the good rub down I'll get in the morning.

I just wish the lady would figure out which treat I like and which canned food I like when I *like them. It IS different every day, but she just can't figure it out. And I wish the man wouldn't kick me off his retirement chair when he wants to use it.*

The lady wrote a children's photo story about me. It's called Purrkins, the Cat. The title is kind of boring, but since it's all about me, it's pretty good.

Magic's Story:

What idiot human would think bunnies like freezing our bunny buns off outside in a small cage? That's how I spent the first part of my life. It wasn't any fun being locked up day and night.

So you might imagine that when I hit the ground at Rose Lake with about 14 of my pals, I was pretty happy. I got to hang out with several female bunnies. One was the creme del a creme. She was a little brown bunny, and I spent three days prancing and hopping about the meadow playing with her.

That was the only good thing about being outside in the real world, though. One really yucky thing was the dead deer that was out there and the maggots, fleas, lice and ticks that seemed to be everywhere. In the course of a couple of days, I felt the crawlies going under my fur, under my skin, and no wiggling and no scratching in the world would keep them off of me. There were also owls and coyotes and other things we had to watch out for, too. In fact, it seemed everything out there wanted to eat us.

I was on my fifth night with my bunny pals and skin parasites, watching out for bad guys when this net went over my head, and I was grabbed by a human and stuck inside a box.

Boxes are scary. Don't let anyone ever tell you otherwise.

When I came back into the light, I was in a pet store where some lady turned me upside down, fondled my genitals, and stuck me back into the box . . . with another male rabbit. How stupid. Darn near got my genitals bitten off.

Way too much later, I was back in the daylight, grabbed by this guy and my wound treated. Later, I was sprayed by this lady with this wet stuff that made me shiver, and I was left in my cage by myself. How rude.

Within minutes of being sprayed, though, I felt the little dark dudes that were imbedded in my skin poke their heads out, pull out the rest of their bodies, and run down my side. One by one, they left me, ran down the cage and out of sight. Meanwhile, other little black hopping things released their hold on me and hopped away. Talk about "eewww." I had nightmares for days afterwards.

The next morning, I ran my feet through my fur and didn't have a single insect on me. As I was grooming, I discovered I was caged next to the little brown bunny. I flirted with her for an hour or so but she ignored me and was taken away soon after. I was moved into my own cage in my own room with this really cheesy carpet that needed to be replaced. I had my own kitten to play with, though, and I mean, who cares if she wasn't a big fuzzy rabbit. She was good enough for me. The kitten's name was Purrkins.

Life was good until I went to this vet, was knocked out and awoke with some very important body parts missing and some teeth gone. I was in so much pain I thought about cashing it in.

But then Purrkins showed up again and nuzzled me with his furry face and told me I needed to get better cuz he missed me. The man came in and said something about how I needed to get better because they had just paid a lot of money to keep me around longer. He covered me up with a towel that smelled good. Then the lady came in and said she loved me and told me she'd get me dandelions and other weeds when I was feeling better. Then she petted me on the head, which I still didn't really like.

So I gave another run at this thing called life, and the lady came true to her word. Sometimes I liked the dandelions, but I mostly just moved them around. I almost always liked the Pop-Tart bit, raisin and vanilla wafers. I got nice and chubby, and after four years, I allowed the lady to pet me. But only sometimes. And only when I felt like it. If I was lying by my water bowl when she came in to see me, I'd let her pet me. If I wasn't, she knew to leave me alone. If she forgot, I'd stomp in my cage.

Purrkins said I had a `tude just like him.

Him? I thought Purrkins was a girl. Oh, no!

Bumpkin's Story:

Riding home on the lady's shoulder in her car was fun and so much better than being inside that shoe box. After I got inside the lady's house, I met her two dogs and a cat, and they didn't scare me at all. I spent my weekdays in the bathroom, my early evenings with the lady eating sunflower shoots and dandelion greens, my evenings with man on the couch or on a towel at his feet. I also had a bath every day and got my own swimming pool. I ruled!

When I had been in the house for a week and a half, I went after the dogs because I knew they had to run away from me or they'd get yelled at, and I ran past the cat to tempt him and he was hissed at, and sometimes I ran the other way when the man tried to get me to go to bed in the bathroom. My "'tude" increased by the day. Soon I came charging out of the bathroom when the door was opened, raced into the kitchen and took over the dog's water dish and food bowl. I liked playing with their food, and eating my own, too, and making a mess of their water. The man and lady had quite a time with me trying to keep me on the towels.

Over time, I shed my downy yellow fuzz and grew white feathers. My peeping became peep-quacking and, finally all quacking. They say I liked to have my way, liked to peck at everything. I guess the male dog didn't like me poking him in his side. I didn't mean to. One day, the lady said she wanted her bathroom back. And her carpeting—which is crazy if you could have seen how lumpy and bad it was.

I got to ride in the back of the Honda Element

all the way to a new place where there were these weird things called ducks. I had to get along with them and hang out with them. They said I was like them. Like a duck. Like that Aflac duck I saw on TV. Only I could fly better than the Aflac duck. A little anyway. Like a brick, the man said. In fact, okay, the only thing close to flying I ever did was riding in the car twice.

At my new home, I got a blue wading pool, lots of duck and chicken pals, a fenced-in pen that goes outside but is covered in chicken wire (why not duck wire?), and a warm toasty barn to sleep in at night. It was a great life for a domestic duck. The new lady and man took to me right away.

My first mom wrote Bumpkin Gets Big, a children's photo story. You should read that, too. There are lots of pictures of me.

BOGO's story:

Sometimes things just don't turn out the way people intend. Take Todd. He lives in Florida and didn't mean to put Mark's name and mailing address on the box that was meant to go to Alabama . . . with me inside. Todd called the Post Office to try to redirect the container, and when Mark learned I was coming, he called the PO, too. But the PO isn't real good at readjusting mid-shipment, and so I ended up in East Lansing where I stayed in my container overnight. In the morning, I was trucked to another small town where a nice guy by the name of Andy called Mark to come pick me up.

When I flew out of my yucky box 38 hours after I left Florida, I was in a small bedroom and saw another bird just like me that Todd had also raised. Its name is Little Buddy. I also saw a whole bunch of these fuzzy things in cages called hamsters, which I'd never seen before.

There was a lady in the room and she looked at me with big bright eyes when I landed on her shoulder. She said she couldn't bear to put me back in the container to ship me to Alabama. So Mark called Todd and said the best thing for me was to stay in Haslett. Luckily, Todd had another baby mynah bird to ship to Alabama, so it all worked out. Mark named me BOGO even though he paid for me.

Little Buddy and I each got our own matching cages, and we get fruit every day and fresh water for baths. Now if only the man and lady would figure out that papayas are only good for a couple of days, whereas bananas—the darker and mushier, the better.

Dusty's Story:
I could have done without the frou-frou bow they put in my hair, and I could have used some Dramamine or a pair of arms to stabilize me for the ride home, but the man and lady didn't know I was prone to car sickness. When I got to their home, they took lots of pictures of me and then took me inside. Early on, Dad said I was the angel pup and was supposed to guard people and take care of animals. I didn't know anything about angels but I did my best anyway to guard

Mom and Dad and all the fuzzies. I liked all of them in their own way.

I still do my best to protect people, warning them of bad guys walking by the house, sitting by Mom at night when she's at the computer, hanging around the bathroom in the morning with a soft, fuzzy toy. Only when Mom goes to the couch at night do I go sit near the bolster. Nobody cares that I can't hear a thing anymore. I'm still the watch dog.

If I could put in a word for one thing, it'd be to tell people to keep their dogs on leashes. We dogs all like to run free at times, but us small dogs are vulnerable. As you know, it only took that one time with that boxer, and I was a mess and in a lot of pain for many days. As I got older, I got more and more afraid of big dogs. Mom carries pepper spray with her when we go on walks; she says it's for a Boogie Man bigger than what I can fight off, but I think it's for dogs, too.

Every critter should get loved and spoiled, but not everyone knows how to go about it. I hope you learned something about that from this book. To learn more, check out mom's photo e-books—they show lots of spoiled, happy pets with fewer words and lots of photos. There's one about me called Dusty, the Angel Pup. You can see it on Mom's web site at www.amylpeterson.com by clicking on My Books. Her site also includes photos of most of the critters in this book.

About the Author

When Amy married Mark in 1994, she became a stepmother to four children ages three, five, 13 and 15. Unable to find uplifting self-help books about step-parenting, Amy documented her own humorous and stressful experience in *From Zero to Four Kids in Thirty Seconds*. Her book includes numerous tips for stepmoms and is a fun, entertaining read.

At the same time Amy was thrown head-first into the world of stepmotherhood, she was also unwittingly plunged into the world of pet ownership. *Something Furry Underfoot* documents Amy's adventures in learning how to care for and spoil a variety pets, and how she ultimately fell for each one. Amy also created four rhyming photo books for kids, each of which tells the story of one of the characters in *Something Furry Underfoot*. A portion of the proceeds from each of Amy's animal books will be donated to animal rescue organizations.

Amy works for the state of Michigan and lives with Mark and numerous critters. When not working or caring for animals, Amy tends to get in trouble while traveling, the details of which may be the basis for her next book.

WANT TO HELP MORE ANIMALS?

Thank you for reading my book! Since a portion of the proceeds from all of my books will be donated to animal rescue organizations, you have already helped to make a difference in the lives of needy pets. If you would like to provide more support to such organizations, please let your friends and family know about my books via email, text messages, Facebook, tweeting or by re-pinning some of my critter photos on Pinterest at http://pinterest.com/amylpeterson. Also, if you liked this book, would you be willing to take a few moments now to write a quick review on Amazon.com or at Smashwords.com? Simply search for Amy L Peterson to find my books. The more books we sell, the more we will help animals in need.

Thank you!

Made in the USA
Lexington, KY
30 December 2013